HOW NOT TO ACT LIKE A *GRUMPY* OLD MAN

by Duncan Rand
Introduction by Mary McHugh

MAGNI

Copyright © 2011 by Magni Group, Inc.

Email: info@magnico.com

ISBN: 978-1-882330-82-9

Manufactured in the United States of America

TABLE OF CONTENTS

INTRODUCTION

Having written, "How Not to Act Like a Little Old Lady" and having lived with a sometimes-cranky old man for many years, I consider myself an expert on grumpy old men, and this is definitely the book to read to keep from being one.

Duncan Rand is decidedly not a grumpy old man and this book gives wonderful advice on how not to be one yourself. He starts off by giving you a long list of things not to do if you don't want to be an old grouch, and then chapter by chapter he tells you ways to ward off the encroachments of age. Really useful things like tricks to help you remember things – I'm highlighting this part in red. Ways to protect your vision and hearing as you get older.

And who would have thought eating healthily could actually be delicious. There's a whole chapter on ways to make fruits and vegetables more tempting than fattening and processed foods. I'm trying his substitute for ice cream – frozen bananas with honey and flavorings mashed up by his wife Phyllis into a creamy delight that tastes heavenly. There's no way you can keep on being a grumpy fat old man after you read this chapter. The real secret to warding off grumpiness as you get older is to keep a little bit of the child in you as you cope with the world. And Duncan Rand's chapter on children and grandchildren shows how much he has kept his own view of life open to new experiences and new perceptions just the way children do. He must be a wonderful father and a grandfather. Especially to Andrea, his granddaughter, who started to cry about something while she was sitting at the table with him and Phyllis, and her grandfather said, "Look out, Andrea. You're going to get your grandmother's tablecloth all wet. Your eyes are leaking." Her frown quickly turned to a smile. What a great way to get a child to stop crying!

It's hard to stay grumpy when you have good friends to share your life with. Duncan's friends are an important part of his life, and he gives you, the reader, some helpful web sites to discover new friends and find old ones in his chapter called "Friends: Old and New".

A crucial part of staying cheerful and non-grumpy as you get older is getting up off your chair and moving. When you read the chapters on sports and exercise, you can't help but follow his advice. If you can't ski and play handball, he says, at least bowl or play badminton or golf or ping-pong. Anything that's fun and keeps you active and limber. Walk, he says, and the way he writes about it, you can't help but follow his advice. You'll want to get out there and breathe the fresh air, Or bicycle. Or swim. Do it! He makes it sound like fun. He's very hard to resist.

You'll discover ways to stay young and eager to try new adventures as you read the chapters on travel, pets, hobbies, computers and cell phones, taking courses, volunteering, marriage, staying positive, a whole list of things still left to do, and wisdom earned throughout a long and positive life with no time for grumpiness.

Mary McHugh

CHAPTER 1:

WHAT IS A GRUMPY OLD MAN?

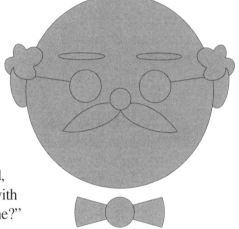

It would be well to start out by identifying a grumpy old man. After all, not everyone in this category may want to admit this is so. Defining the term will help dispel any doubt in your mind if you indeed fit this classification. If you bought this book yourself, that's a sure admission of guilt. But if you received it via your wife or a friend, you might just be resentfully wrestling with the idea and saying to yourself "Who, me?"

It's a sure sign you're grumpy when you:

Complain to your wife about what those little green flakes are on the potatoes—particularly when the little green flakes don't really taste bad at all.

Make complaints about the food with a full mouth. —What if you had to cook it yourself?

Curse when you spill a spoonful of food that you have to clean up yourself because your wife is out of town—even when it falls on an easy to clean surface.

Curse when you spill a few drops of drink that you have to clean up yourself because your wife is out of town—even when it falls on an easy to clean surface.

Fail to excuse a belch at the table—especially an uncovered one!

Restrict your vocabulary to "Yes, Dear" at the breakfast table—and say them in an unbecoming tone.

Blame the manufacturer when you have difficulty opening a jar of pickles bare-handed—even though a rubber gripper is within easy reach.

Dress in soiled clothing. —If only *they* could clean *you*. (Or should it be said, "clean *up*" on you?)

Throw your clothes on the floor. —If only the clothes could talk.

Yell at the referees or umpires on the TV screen. —If only they could here you.

Slam the door—particularly when all isn't going badly at all.

Shoo the neighborhood kids off your front lawn—even when they are generating little or no noise.

Chew out the Misses for over spending—especially when the items purchased are pure necessities.

Chide your wife for spending on a new dress—even after you just bought a second external hard drive for the computer solely because the store was willing to let it go at a deep discount.

Snap at the little lady for gossiping—although you are unable to make an exact count of number of times you were guilty of the same thing.

Make exclamations every time you set eyes on the bills—even ones with reasonable figures.

Criticize the government for the state of the economy—when you have more than you've ever had.

Fuss about a tax increase—although the figures on your bank account are higher than they ever have been.

Hold animosity for all drivers who get ahead of you in traffic—or even just a few of them.

Lean on the horn whenever the driver whose stopped in front of you doesn't immediately respond to a green traffic signal—even when you have the rest of the day free and you're only 2 blocks from home.

Bang the computer monitor every time a program crashes—even if what you are doing involves play as opposed to serious work.

Ignore the little woman during a TV program—even when it's not the best of breed.

Spout off about the high volume of TV commercials—when you own a DVR and can record the programs and skip past the commercials when you play them back.

Criticize the mail carrier for being late—even though you expect nothing of importance.

Criticize the newspaper carrier for being late—even though you have all day to read the news.

Think mean thoughts about the neighbor who awakes you because of an early-morning lawn mowing session—although you have plenty of time for sleep.

Kick the refrigerator for conking out with a full load of food just purchased at the biggest bargain of the year. —If only that 'fridge could immediately start running again, this time out of the house and away from you forever.

Register loud protest when the air conditioning goes out to lunch in the middle of the summer—despite the fact that the weather is the mildest on record.

Ball out your wife for talking too much—even though you may talk more than her.

Gripe about the garbage collectors for arriving ahead of schedule and beating you to the punch—when you have one of the lightest loads of trash in recent family history.

Get angry at a cranky window shade—If only that shade could tell you how cranky *you* are.

Don't bother to shave for 3 days—even though your wife has reminded you 3 times each day.

Bark back at the dog. —Oh, how Fido bounces back, but it hurts at the moment.

Bark (worse still) at the cat. —If only Mittens could trade places for about 5 minutes.

CHAPTER 2:

THE FACTS OF (SENIOR) LIFE

As Mary McHugh said in her book, *How Not to Act Like a Little Old Lady,* "How the heck did I get to be this old?" Wasn't it just an hour or so ago that I was an active, on-the-go individual, still working, viewing retirement as something to look forward to, but which seemed would never really come? That, however, doesn't matter now. The fact is that I find myself a member of the senior citizen's club, try as I may to put it out of my mind.

As you well know, there are a number of unpleasant concerns that grip you at this time of life. Your vision has dimmed; your auditory senses have diminished; your memory has faded; your hair has grayed and thinned; your equilibrium has become cock-eyed, your grip is weaker, your strength has ebbed—the spring in your step having taken a powder. Your new companions are aches and pains, along with an broader assortment of medications (expensive, to say the least)—as well as heating pads, hot water bottles, inner soles and maybe even dentures. You realize you're making more visits to the doctor and less to places you would like to go. On top of everything else, you've even shrunk vertically and quite probably expanded horizontally.

There is no use denying it. If we live long enough, we have to face a slower pace (pun fully intentional). Furthermore, it's not just the classic case of the brain saying "go" but the body saying "no"—far too often the brain steps out to lunch and then is late getting back. It's an experience with which I am quite familiar. The least little distraction, such as a telephone call or a question from my wife, Phyllis, will throw me off stride and a moment later it's: "Let's see, what was I doing?"

It's a scenario that can best be summed up by the old joke in which the question is posed to a senior citizen, "Do you ever wonder about the hereafter?"

and his response, "Do I ever. I go into one room and then another room and wonder what I'm here after."

Now you find yourself a grumpy individual over it all, if not obnoxious or downright ornery. I know. I've been there. Odds are that if you took a peek at yourself in the mirror, other than at a time when you are shaving (and making faces that distort a representation of the real you), you might just catch the outline of an upside down smile.

As long as there was a 6 as the first digit of your age, it probably didn't seem so bad. Even 69 might not have appeared to be any scarier than 61. You might even have made a joke on your 69th birthday (complete with an appropriate chuckle) that you were 69 and holding. But then the day arrived (in rather sneaky fashion) and you found yourself staring straight into a number larger than one that fit your comfort level: 70 or 70-something, if not 80 or more, and slapped suddenly with the concept that your future was slipping out the door. But does this mean life has turned sour? Can't your days still be full of joy, adventure, friends, laughter, learning and accomplishment?

I'm here to tell you that it can, that things really aren't so bad after all, that you have permission to smash the set-in-stone notion that high age figures are black magic numbers that equate to be being put out to pasture—and beyond a twelve-foot barbed wire fence, at that. You are only old in the number of years you've lived—not necessarily in the way you think, talk and act.

It's encouraging to note that although the cells of the human body have short lives, they reproduce prolifically—and that includes brain cells. In fact, our bodies produce 100,000 new brain cells every day, no matter how old we get. So provided you don't get flattened by a Mack truck, this continual regeneration makes it possible to keep going mentally as well as physically.

That alone should entice you to seek the positive rather than the negative, accept challenge rather than giving up, reach out instead of withdrawing. It may not all be down hill in the shade with a pocket full of goodies, but there are silver linings on a many a cloud and lots of clear days to boot.

If nothing else at the moment, you can take heart in the fact that you are not alone. There's a many millions of us in this country, 10's of millions over 80 alone. Then add the fact that people are living longer these days.

That's a good start. But there is a lot more. However, before I get too far along, I want to make sure you are fully aware of the facts surrounding senior life. Confronting them in more specific terms will help you fully realize what you're up against. Then, hopefully, it will be easier to shear the bonds of grumpiness and cope more gracefully. If you are of age, expect to:

- Cup your hand to your ear a lot more, or to say "hmm" more frequently.

- No longer see the specks on the floor that your granddaughter does—at least not without *your* specks.

- See spots dancing before the pages of a book you are reading—a dance step that is not particularly appealing.

- Have trouble keeping your eyes on the words while reading.

- Turn up the volume on the TV.

- Turn up the volume on the radio.

- Turn up the lights.

- Be shorter of breath

- No longer have to identify yourself as a senior when you're being charged at a restaurant.

- Groan when you rise from you easy chair.

- Hear a creak when you rise from your easy chair that doesn't originate with the chair.

- Grunt when you rise from a squat.

- Become unable to squat at all.

- Do more sitting.

- Do more laying around.

- Give a lot more advice than you are taking.

- Increase the number of visits to the doctor by no less than 33 1/3%.

- Take more medicine.

- Discover more foods that disagree with you.

- Sustain more injuries.

- Find more cuts and bruises that take longer to heal.

- Make more frequent trips to the bathroom.

- Become acquainted with a new pain.

- Notice a thinner chest and rounder belly.

- Misplace more of your possessions more often.

- Get rattled every time there is an unexpected change in routine—even if it turns out for the better.

- Discover that the length of a month now seems more like that of a week.

- Hear more words in the English language with which you are not familiar.

- Move slower than your brain is telling you to.

- Miss rather than hit what you're aiming for at least 25% more of the time.

- Increase the amount of times you drop things.

- Seek your grandchildren's advice about the operation of electronic equipment, such as cell phones.

- Screw jar lids on crooked.

- Spill more—especially on surfaces that have just been cleaned.

- Forget more—even after vowing you will remember.

- Lose your balance more readily.

- Find certain doors and drawers more difficult to open.

- Be proud of yourself when you change a tire—even if you had help.

- Discover that making simple repairs are more of a challenge—if you ever were inclined toward repair.

- More frequently miss the point in a conversation.

- Avoid stooping—even if already half stooped from a bad back.

- Spit more.

- Cough more.

- Sneeze more.

- Clear your throat more.

- Brag when you have a good bowel movement.

- Find you have shrunk.

- Double the amount of times you miscount.

- Get more clumsy.

- Use your hanky more.

- Double check on yourself more—and find you're glad you did..

- Cut your activities in half.

- Go to bed earlier.

- And, of course, become grumpy.

There's more. But isn't that enough? The big question is: "What can we do about any of it?" And even if we must resign ourselves to every difficulty, "How can we avoid being grumpy over the matter?" Move over to the next page and I'll show you how.

CHAPTER 3:

SENIOR PATCHES

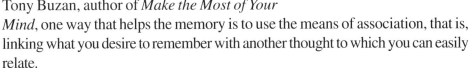

Your life might not be as lively or as rosy anymore, but that doesn't mean you can't improve matters somewhat. Before you throw up your hands in despair, consider these helpful facts that I've learned throughout the years.

You can give yourself a memory upgrade—and it can even be fun to do so. According to Tony Buzan, author of *Make the Most of Your Mind*, one way that helps the memory is to use the means of association, that is, linking what you desire to remember with another thought to which you can easily relate.

It works this way. Say you want to remember the name of the neighbor's friend you just met. If the name happens to be Fred Pomeroy, you might, perhaps, picture a big red "F" (F plus red) dangling from a palm tree or your cousin Fred seated beneath it. Should the name be Mary Parker, your great grandson's school teacher, just think of the *merry* time you had when you were *parked* at that out-of-the-way spot with your first girl. Get the idea?

But what if you needed to remember the following list of unrelated items?

Antenna	Golf Club
Swan	Heaven
Traffic signal	Hour glass
Sailboat	Pipe
Fishing hook	Hen

It's not nearly as difficult as you think when you attach numbers to the list. Now examine the list again.

1. Antenna	6. Golf Club
2. Swan	7. Heaven
3. Traffic Signal	8. Hourglass
4. Sailboat	9. Pipe
5. Fishing hook	10. Hen

Understand the pattern? See how each number corresponds to the word after it? An antenna is contoured like the number 1, a 2 emulates a swan, a traffic signal has lights of 3 colors, a 4 resembles the sail of a boat, etc. The word "breast" could have just as easily been substituted for the term "traffic signal" in number 3, just as number 7 could have the word "cliff" after it, rather than "heaven", which rhymes with 7 and is often associated with it. Likewise, 10 could just as easily be a bat and a ball, rather than "hen", as in the nursery rhyme "9, 10, a big fat hen."

By the same token, 12 could be associated with eggs, since you buy them by the dozen, 45 could be a reminder of the word "records," since there used to be 45 rpm records. (Remember them? If you don't, you have no reason to be reading this book!)

So why not play the association game at the next opportunity. The next time your wife asks you to pick up tomatoes, bread and milk at the corner market, just picture a tomato sandwich floating in a giant bottle of milk. And if you want to remember that you have an appointment with your cardiologist, Dr. Curtis, Wednesday at 10 on March 18th, picture a 1 curtsying to a 0 before their wedding day and then watch as they march off, happy that there are of age (18), or some other such nonsense.

I find this strategy useful to me. Sometimes, however, I fall into laziness and neglect to take advantage of it. But when I make the effort, it usually works.

As far as the mental side of things is concerned, it is also a good idea to read a lot. I think it helps keep the mind sharp. I knew an elderly man who read profusely and he remained sharp witted until the day of his death—at 96.

What about your vision? Don't throw away your eyeglasses, but here are some tips I know that might help improve your ability to see.

First, don't neglect the obvious. Keep those eyeglasses clean. (You do *wear* glasses, don't you?)

Tension has a negative effect on vision by straining the eyes. Make an effort to relax.

Often, a healthy body equates to healthy vision. So take care of your health. Maintain a well-balanced diet, get plenty of fresh air, enough exercise and adequate sleep.

Make sure you are blinking enough. That's right. Often when we become more intent on something we are looking at for lengthy periods (such as when we read), we place ourselves in a staring mode and unconsciously neglect blinking, which results in eyestrain.

By the same token, breathing is often affected under the same circumstance. Intense concentration leads to erratic breathing. You may even sometimes catch yourself holding your breath under such circumstances. I know I have. Make certain you inhale and exhale at a regular tempo and that your breathing is relaxed.

When reading or doing intricate work, opt for sunlight streaming though a window whenever possible, rather than relying on a lamp. Natural light is always better for the eyes. (Always avoid fluorescent light. It casts very little shadow, which sharply reduces contrast, making it particularly hard on the eyes.)

I try to do most of my reading during the day when I have full light from my back room that has plenty of windows. The eyestrain is much less than when I'm reading under a lamp at night. In fact, as long as I have access to sunlight, I don't need glasses to see every word clearly—even small type. I get along this way well unless there is a thick overcast.

Rest your eyes when the opportunity avails itself. Do this by palming, that is, close your eyes and cup your hands over them, forming a dome. Then try to imagine a pure black background. I've done this lots of times and it does help rest the eyes.

I've discovered that the longer you do this, the better the effect. Once when I was in bed sick with the flu, I put it to the test. I was so feverish, I didn't even feel like reading or watching TV. All I craved was quiet. So I devoted a considerable amount of time on the routine, draping a dark cloth over my eyes to make matters easier.

The next day, I was doing much better and got out of bed to continue my normal routine. I was amazed how much clearer by vision was. I get the impression that if one stayed with it long enough (without dying of boredom), he would soon be able to toss his reading glasses. Any volunteers?

As far as the ears are concerned, treat them like you would a sophisticated musical instrument. (You musicians can appreciate that.) They should not be abused. Avoid close and sustained contact with things that generate loud noise, such as heavy machinery. I've always been able to do this, and I guess it's paid. I wish my vision was still as efficient as my auditory senses.

Try to become a better listener. Concentrate on tuning out distractions by focusing more intensely on what is being said. And if what you are hearing is boring, try to find something interesting about it. (This may prove exasperating if your wife is relating every moment she experienced at the beauty shop that morning, and you might have to intrigue yourself with the challenge of unearthing at least one stimulating fact, at least until you've succeeded in changing the subject.)

If you have already sustained ear damage and are having a particularly difficult time hearing, there is an option. You undoubtedly own a pair of eyeglasses to assist your vision, so paste a band-aid over your ego and invest in a hearing aid.

As far as thinning hair goes, there's nothing wrong with a toupee. And for the color gray, scientists have come up with an amazing development—dye!

CHAPTER 4:

EATING YOUR WAY TO BETTER HEALTH

One thing that becomes particularly crucial in later years is the matter of health. After enough aches and pains, we tend to become more health-conscious, and that, fortunately, convinces us to take better care of ourselves. I had the good fortune of being aware of this early on in life and I believe it has helped me preserve a better state of health.

We need adequate exercise, plenty of fresh air (that lets out smoking), and enough sleep. We also need to learn how the respond favorably to stress. But particularly important to our state of health are our eating habits.

Prior to the age of about 30, I had the bad habit of eating sweet rolls for breakfast. And I didn't stop there. As far as I was concerned, it was inconceivable to partake of a meal without rich desserts and soft drinks with which to wash them down. And there was always room for a snack at night, as if I didn't get enough at dinner, which consisted almost exclusively of more of the same junk food. Pretty soon, these kind of foods became the centerpiece of every repast.

One day I got the bold notion of switching up my routine and substituting fresh fruit, such as oranges and melons, for the sweet rolls, cupcakes, pie, cookies, ice cream and other unhealthful victuals. I just thought I ought to give myself a change for once—just for that one day.

And guess what? I never went back. I felt so different, so much more alive, energetic, that I realized what I had been doing to my body. In fact, I had so much extra energy from continuing my new diet that I used some of it to start growing a garden. Then I had even more nourishing food to add to my diet. And not only did

I maintain that energy level, I lost weight too. I'm so grateful I learned this early on. Interesting how things can turn out for the good.

You probably know the score, but here is basically what constitutes a healthy diet:

- Eat plenty of fruits and vegetables, particularly of the raw variety. They are specifically designed for the human body. (Be aware, however, that certain foods, such as dark green leafy vegetables—ordinarily very healthful—are not to be consumed if you are you are on certain medications. Check with your doctor about this.)

- Avoid heavily processed foods, such as potato chips, cookies and pies. They may be high in fat content and they contain refined sugar and additives.

- Shun fatty foods. Cut down or eliminate red meat from your diet, as well as any other packaged foods that list a high quantity of fat on the label.

- Reduce your intake of fried foods. Oils must be used in the process and all are fattening.

- Don't overeat. That only taxes the digestive system and contributes to your weight. (And being fat doesn't necessarily equate to being jolly.)

One other fact I've learned that I want to point out is that some foods believed to be fattening by many are not at all, only what is added to them. A prime example is a baked potato. It has virtually no fat calories, but not so for the butter, sour cream and bacon bits that are often used as toppings. And there's certainly no way you are going to gain excess pounds eating spinach. But cream spinach is another matter, since it contains cheese.

Over the years, I've become even more health conscious and made it a habit to eat a higher volume of raw foods. This has not only enabled me to feel even better, but I have noticed a side benefit. My teeth have gotten whiter. It has made me realize just how effective raw foods are in cleaning the teeth.

You might think that sticking to a healthy diet is difficult. But it doesn't have to be. Habits are hard to break, but as I learned, you can turn that fact to your advantage. Once I stopped my old eating habits and begin a cleaner diet, I had established a new habit pattern, and once I did, I found *it* was just as hard to break.

It reminds me of my grandfather, who, when I was just a toddler, made a new year's resolution to stop smoking. On the first of that year, he placed the fresh cigars he had remaining in a can and put it on a shelf in front of the kitchen window. They sat there until they had begun to deteriorate and my grandmother had to throw them out. I don't know how he succeeded by keeping them in front of him that way. But that demonstrates what one can do who sets his mind to it.

I'm not suggesting you make it harder on yourself by keeping food that's bad for you around the house. You'll be wanting to eat it and you surely will. Develop the habit of purchasing more healthful foods (or tell your wife to) and they will be around when you're ready to eat them.

Now to help you get the ball rolling, think about this. Our society has developed the opinion that if it's good for you it doesn't taste good, and if it's bad for you, it's automatically delicious. The fact is: You can make anything taste appealing, just as you can make anything to taste bad. If you were to roll a cookie in the dirt, you wouldn't want to eat it, but if a serving of green beans was laced with a lively seasoning, your taste buds would likely be appreciative. Bear this in mind and you will rid yourself of the aforementioned prejudice. You will be encouraged to make healthful foods taste more appealing so you will want to eat them.

Here are some tips I've learned for making sure that food tastes good, which you can pass on to the little woman (unless you have the meal preparation chore yourself):

Take full advantage of spices. Use the ones you like best (and, of course, the ones that don't bother your digestion). There are plenty of seasoning choices, such as: red pepper; lemon pepper; curry; oregano; paprika; garlic powder; turmeric; celery salt; nutmeg; ginger; allspice; cream of tartar; butter sprinkles; cheese sprinkles; not to mention plain, ordinary salt and pepper. And don't forget about onions and garlic. You don't always have to use them in cooking, some can be applied to raw foods as well.

I've often found that a little sea salt and red pepper liven up an avocado. Sometimes I even sprinkle on a spoonful of wheat germ. And I love plenty of oregano on my spaghetti. Garlic is also welcomed or a slice of onion on the side. I've enjoyed dill seed in potato salad, too, and garlic powder on various vegetables. I also go light on butter, often replacing it with butter flakes (goes good on popcorn). You can also include butter flavoring in cooked dishes (if you're not familiar, a liquid in a bottle just like vanilla extract).

There are also a number of healthful, yet enjoyable substitutions. We've used honey or fruit juices with few or no added ingredients in recipes instead of refined sugar. And we also use honey for a spread rather than jam or jelly. We have replaced candy with dried fruits, such as raisins, dates, figs and pineapple. I call dates "God's candy." I love those little devils as much as I ever did any kind of confection. Figs are a close second in my book and they, like prunes, have the added advantage of assisting with that certain bathroom activity just as efficiently as wheat bran. In fact, I've overdone it on several occasions, so be careful.

I have long since given up ice cream, so I have Phyllis mash up servings of bananas, add honey and a little flavoring, and freeze them in little containers. Bananas are a good choice because they provide a thicker, smoother texture that more closely emulates cream. There are lots of extracts I've sampled with this cool treat besides vanilla; namely, cherry, coconut, almond, anise (derived from a plant of the carrot family and tasting like licorice), lemon, and strawberry. Sometimes I get surprised and find slices of other fruits included, such as peach or strawberry. (Between you and me, I think those times are when she has run out of flavorings. I have never bothered to inquire. And it's not as though I don't like banana, either.)

Avocados make a good substitute for eggs. Both foods contain fat, but the fat in avocados does not contain animal fat, which I try to avoid so I can better keep my weight down. Although of a totally different color, their flavor resembles that of the hen fruit. If I close my eyes while eating, I hardly know the difference.

And here's one more point. Beverages are just as important as the food we eat. What we drink, then, should be nourishing too. Any fresh fruit or vegetable drinks are the most healthful. Homemade are the best because they will be the freshest. We've liquefied bananas, strawberries and other fruits in a blender, and they are delicious. They resemble a milk shake and that thicker consistency makes them more satisfying. I like to blend fresh pineapple with coconut flavoring. That way, I get the benefit of the coconut flavor without the fat from the coconut itself (not that it should be that bad health-wise since it's not animal fat).

I also enjoy a tall glass of homemade tomato juice once in a while. But I've found that it doesn't work very well when we blend it with other combinations, so I just drink it by itself. Sometimes we go ahead and buy it at the store.

Another exceptionally healthful drink that I have grown to enjoy is carrot juice. Sometimes we make it from fresh carrots and sometimes we just purchase it at the market. What I like about it is its effect on me. I've noticed a remarkable rise in my energy level and increased respiratory function within a half-hour to an hour after consuming it.

These drinks are great along with a healthful meal. If you put your imagination to work, you will undoubtedly come up with more ideas for preparing meals that better suit your taste. You'll be encouraged once you feel the positive effects of a more healthful diet. It might have more impact than you think and you could even find your arthritis isn't troubling you as much or your back pain has eased off.

I could go on, but my publisher wouldn't want the "tome" you're holding to veer away from the subject at hand.

CHAPTER 5:

GRANDCHILDREN AND GREAT GRANDCHILDREN

There's nothing that will take your mind off what makes you grumpy like times with grandchildren or great grandchildren, as the case may be. When else would you get the chance to play ball or cops and robbers (you being the robber, of course), or swing in the park or whisper sweet somethings (or is it sweet *nothings*) into the ear of a that special person's favorite doll.

If you still have young grandchildren, you are starring straight into a second chance to recapture your childhood. If you now have great grandchildren (Guess what?), you have a third chance. Take advantage. While you're teaching them, learn from observation. Try to pick up on their carefree-ness. Let them help you unwind.

Some of the things they say are amusing, as you probably well know. For instance, there was the time I was in charge of my nephew, who posed a very pertinent question at the most opportune moment. We were just passing an ice cream store when he asked, "Grand Daddy, have I been good today?"

There are lots of loving and amusing moments when it comes to the younger breed. For the record, here's a brief quote list—some relating to my own experience; some which others have shared with me. Do any of them sound familiar?

"Grand Daddy, watch this!" while he proceeds to complete a lopsided cartwheel.

"Why are leaves green?" She asks with ruffled brow, eyeing the big oak tree.

"I'm gon'na grow up to be just like Grandpa." (You're setting a good example, aren't you?)

"What's that little thing that hangs down between Spot's legs?" (Of course, you've already been through all that with your children, now grown and explaining it to their children.)

"Can't we stay just a little longer?" (when it's getting dark at the park and you know you're going to catch it from the little woman if you don't get back)

"Grandpapa, do that one more time." (After you make a face that you hope won't freeze into place)

"Can't I have just one more teeny weeny piece of cake, Nanny," she says, holding out two rounded fingers to indicate just how much "teeny weeny" is.

"Why do they call this piggyback, instead of people-back?"

"Grampa, get that bug," she gasps, with her legs drawn up in the chair, while squinting at a wadded up rubber band across the room.

"Can't I just have one more chance?" he pleads, after his crayon slips along the wall—several times.

"Can't we do this again tomorrow?"

"Nanny, can we lick the bowl?" she asks eagerly as the cake batter is being poured into the pan for cooking.

"I want to spend the night with Grandy and Big Mommy!" he exclaims with cocked head while seated in his grandfather's lap.

"I'm glad you and Granddad came to see us."

"Don't tell Mommy! Please?" As much with her eyes as with her mouth. (After spilling milk on the table)

"I got'ta get things looking spark-and-speak," the enthusiastic little helper says while wiping the table top, rather than "spick-and-span."

"Listen, everybody, I have a speech-ment to make," as he extends his hands during a family gathering.

"Grand Daddy, your breath smells so good. What did you put on it?"

"This is the most delicious kind of fish I ever ate," he declares with smacking mouth, as he chomps on a hush puppy.

"Granpaps, would you make my kite quit flying?"

"Grandma, would you open my banana?"

And, of course, that famous line, "I love you."

Children have taken my mind off the stressful things in my life on many occasions. I probably felt the impact of this more than any other time when I used to take Andrea, my granddaughter (then about 3 years old), to ride the "horsey." We would get in the car, just the two of us, and drive down to the mall, where not far inside the entrance was one of those rocking horses—you know—the kind you drop a dime in to make it go. Yes, all of one thin dime. But it would cost me 20 cents, invariably, because she'd always talk me into a second ride. (Her wistful blue eyes were irresistible.) We would drive back, her standing up in the front seat (long before the seat belt law, of course), fully satisfied at having attained her fix. I've made sure my grandson, Richard, has also received the privilege of such rides, but Andrea seemed to most intent about it.

I have also given my grandchildren something to remember besides horse rides several times during the winter months when sleet had iced over the streets. I let them sit in a wooden box on which a rope was attached, and pulled them along the sidewalk. They wanted more than I could give them, but they loved what they got.

I'll never forget my granddaughter's reaction at a family birthday party for my uncle one spring. She had become unhappy about some minor incident, one of those matters that was of colossal proportions to a 6-year-old, and began to cry during dinner.

I said to her, "Look out, Andrea. You're going to get your grandmother's tablecloth all wet. Your eyes are leaking."

Her frown quickly turned to a smile, whereupon she covered her mouth because she didn't want to abandon her spirit of protest. But that little towhead couldn't escape the fact that her sadness had been drowned out.

We were at the amusement park one summer when that same little girl accompanied by my grandson, Richard, and myself on a ride on the mini roller coaster. She had hesitated, but Richard kept teasing her about missing some real fun if she didn't. She finally relented on the condition that I ride along with them, so that was the reason I had joined the party. She began to have reservations as the ride progressed, and I was beginning to regret that she hadn't elected to sit this one out. The ride ended in a dramatic climax with 3 big dips, and that got her. She began to cry.

As we got off and proceeded down the midway, I gave her a reassuring hug, but she hadn't let up.

"What's the matter, Honey?" I finally asked. "You're off the thing now."

In answer, she squalled, "I swallowed my gum!"

Richard burst forth with a big cackle and I almost got the hiccups suppressing a laugh.

I recall another incident worth sharing related to me by my daughter, Jan, when her son, Richard, was ill with the flu. The doctor, after having administered a shot, had only just left. (They were still making house calls then.) Suddenly, my grandson appeared, fully clothed, at the kitchen door where his mother was scrubbing the cabinets. "What are you doing out of bed, young man?" she demanded to know, whereupon he asked, "Didn't the doctor make me well?"

And how about the little accomplishments, gigantic in the eyes of the young? I had the privilege of perusing the first picture that Andrea drew in school, a lady dancer in green with a tall hat, complete with the teacher's addition in the form of a gold star. She sat there in my lap, with that distinct smell of the skin that only children possess, her eyes reflecting that proud demeanor as if it was a di Vinci masterpiece.

I was there when Richard caught his first fish, the size of which made me fear it could almost have been lost in the jaws of an overgrown minnow. I was a bona fide witness, too, when he took his initial bicycle ride without training wheels.

Sometimes children will do those innocent little things that don't set well with parents, or grandparents, as the case may be. Once the neighbor's Kerry blue terror had wondered into our yard and Phyllis looked out the kitchen window to see Andrea, who we had been baby-sitting, busily picking rice off the animal's whiskers and eating the grains one by one. This was, of course, right after she had been served a sandwich that she had only half finished. (That was the same girl that had slipped out the door with it earlier and managed to hold it by one corner without spilling any of its contents, the same little tyke who would hold her spoon in her left hand like a knife and turn it upside down as she brought food to her mouth without hardly ever spilling a morsel.) What made matters of special concern was that she had just recovered from the flu. You can imagine how fast my wife moved to end that session.

Of course, there are those tense, trying moments as well. Once Richard was sent to get a haircut and requested that the barber leave a thick strip of hair down the middle of his head. He came home looking like a Mohawk Indian, or maybe that should be Mohegan. Jan was hopping mad over it.

She said, "This is worse than the time the Sunday School teacher caught him squirting water from the church rest room lavatories."

I told her later that at least he didn't get off to school that way, and that it was better than if he had been smoking or doing drugs.

That was more easily repairable than what my neighbor's son did to himself. He painted his arms green so he could pretend he was the Incredible Hulk. Fortunately, he never got to his face with the paint before he was stopped. (That was the same boy, by the way, who took an ink pen to both his hands when he was younger and had a field day drawing little men on his palms and fingers—just after he had been given a bath.)

Sometimes things can get more serious. Several years back, my neighbor across the street built his young grandson a go-cart. It was against his better judgment, but the boy (who found it next to impossible to recognize "no" as a word in the English language) had kept after him for weeks. On the next visit, he unveiled the new toy and the boy was delighted to give it a trial run. After the engine was cranked up and he got started, he rode down the sidewalk, circled into the street and headed back, turning into the driveway with his foot still affixed firmly to the gas pedal. He had frozen. Somehow he pulled himself together and hit the brake just before smashing into the garage.

Other times, things get even more serious. My neighbor once related an incident to me when he and his wife were in the process of replacing a mattress. Against their better judgment, they allowed their 6-year-old son and 4-year-old daughter to bounce on the old mattress that had been placed on the floor beside the bed. All was well for the first few minutes. Then their son got too close to the edge and hit his head on a dresser handle. He jumped up screaming in pain, blood running down his back. The wound wasn't nearly as severe as it first appeared, but it obviously hurt. Meanwhile, his daughter somehow envisioned the matter as humorous and my neighbor was soon spanking her for laughing, while his wife applied medical aid.

Unfortunately, that wasn't the only injury the boy sustained that year. Later that summer, he fell when he was trying to climb a stop sign pole and skinned both knees. The next year, he fell out of a tree house and broke his collarbone.

In a stymied line at the bank one summer, I overheard a woman relating the following to a companion. She had left her son in the living room with a coloring book while mopping the kitchen floor. Soon her nostrils detected a suspicious odor—one that was not originating from the mop bucket. She looked up not surprised to see an unattended coloring book and crayons. At the same instant she was bolting toward the bathroom, knowing full well what she would find. Sure enough, he had seen fit to reposition the knob on the gas heater a mere quarter of a turn and proceeded to his room to roll around his toy fire engine. After she got things under control, she followed up with a stern reprimand, thinking about how close she had come to seeing a *real* fire engine.

To celebrate her birthday, the family once treated Andrea and her friends to a session of roller skating. I believe she had one of the best times she ever did. But that night she experienced excruciating pain and Jan and my son-in-law, Gerald, feared appendicitis. They rushed her to the emergency only to learn that the pain had been induced by muscle strain from too many turns on the skating rink.

One time, Richard and I had planned a fishing trip for just for the two of us and he was especially eager to go. I had played it up all morning long. We had put the fishing gear in order and packed a lunch, and were just about to leave. He then proceeded to walk out the door, the sliding glass variety, that lead out to the detached garage—only the door wasn't open. Replacing the door was the least of my worries at the moment. I was faced with a child who had acquired a body full of cuts and bruises, who asked simply, "Does this mean we don't get to go fishing?"

I'll not forget the time he got turned around in an out-of-town amusement park. It was getting dark, and the family had covered just about the whole grounds before we spotted him, ironically wandering not far from where he had become lost. His moist eyes and swollen cheeks told of a brave little boy who tried his darndest to keep from crying. As it turned out, wind had blown dust into his eyes. (If you believe that, I have a whole sea to sell you cheap—the Sea of Tranquillity—on the moon!)

At such times you are especially glad to see them, just as it was when 6-year-old Andrea jumped in the our car, put it into gear and calmly drove away. I was panic stricken for a few minutes—until I awoke to discover it was nothing more than a nightmare. Her and my grandson were due for a visit that very day and you can imagine how I felt about seeing her.

Sometimes the little ones ask questions that you would rather not have to answer at the moment. I'm not just talking about the birds and the bees. Once when my wife and I had charge of the grand kids, we were driving home from an amusement park. Actually, it had been one of those portable assemblage of rides temporarily brought in by a group that had leased a vacant lot. It was the last day before they were to close shop and we didn't want the kids to miss out, especially since we had already promised. The weather had been overcast and somewhat threatening, but that didn't deter us. However, when conditions had begun to deteriorate substantially, we thought it best to head back. It was a challenge to pull Richard off the Ferris wheel. Riding it had been the nearest thing to being an airline pilot, he had informed me.

As we were driving back home, it had started to rain. Andrea, faced toward the back window, pointed, and innocently asked, "Grand Daddy, what's that?"

I looked into the rearview mirror only the set sight on a tornado.

"It's something we don't want to get into," was my initial response as I speeded up, while observing its direction of travel. Fortunately, the funnel never touched ground and the storm, headed adjacent to us quickly dissipated. But it was a big question and I took the time to fully elaborate on it after we arrived safe and sound.

There are times when you turn out to be quite the hero. I've repaired the hand brake on my granddaughter's bike, for instance, and secured the loose wire that enabled my grandson to play his crystal radio set. I didn't always get "thank you's" for things like that (the take-it-for-granted syndrome, you know), but I was graced with them on those two occasions as well as a number of others and considered that a pretty good track record.

Then there are those little peculiarities. When she was very young, Andrea developed a fear of gloves. As long as someone was wearing them, all was fine. But take them off, and it was horrors. Once Phyllis dropped one in the dining room and she avoided it as though it was a swarming beehive. And a neighbor once told me of a child who was afraid of his parent's toaster. He would never come any closer than necessary to the kitchen cabinet where it was resting when breakfast was being served. And he never wanted toast. I wonder what his attitude was toward a jack-in-the-box?

Children are indeed a special breed and I wonder how anyone could find reason to abuse one. There's nothing to compare with their bright, refreshing eyes; their cute giggles, and that unique laugh when being tickled. And there is that boundless energy that would go a long way toward reducing your electric bill if it could only be converted into electricity.

That energy instead is sometimes pointed in another direction (although pro-pelled by good intention), as when I had made the idle statement that my car needed a paint job within earshot my young nephew. Later that afternoon I was short about a half gallon of Colonial yellow paint and held the distinct privilege of owning a blue Chevy with a yellow left front fender. Needless to say, I wasn't very happy, but my wife tempered the matter a bit by reminding me that it was a good thing that I didn't also get a free fill up via the garden hose.

Usually such circumstances are not that teeth-grinding, as in the case of the eager helper who is attempting to pour from a pitcher of iced tea seemingly as big as her, while you hold your breath—or the little boy who is spreading more leaves than he is raking. It's the kind of energy that is magically diverted to other matters when you actually ask for the help.

But even with the trials, isn't it nice to have them around? Especially when you realize that childhood is like a rose. It's beautiful while it lasts, but it will all too soon be gone.

And here's a touching scene to close the chapter. I'll never forget the time I watched my 90-year-old grandmother walking down the front sidewalk in hand with my 2-year-old niece, both unsteady of foot—generations apart, yet as close as love could bring them. That would make an excellent painting, wouldn't you say?

CHAPTER 6:

FRIENDS: OLD AND NEW

Friends play a big part in the later years of life. Oh, they can be annoying at moments and misunderstanding can surface, such as the time when I was fresh out of college and a friend wore out his welcome by always managing to drop in at dinner time or when I was ready for bed. But friends are an asset, and even as in the above case, it gives one the blessed opportunity to patch things up, which we promptly did.

I have learned that a really good friend has a way of being there when you need him. One example in my life is Ken. I knew him way back when we were kids and he lived next door to me. We built playhouses, went to movies, wrestled until one of us said "uncle" and got into general mischief together. One time we even connected a pair of toy telephones from his bedroom to mine and established a free, but rather unreliable, private line.

Once when Phyllis was out of town visiting her sister in Rochester and I promptly sprained my ankle, Ken had no misgivings about coming over to be my temporary crutch. I'd made a misstep on my front sidewalk, but I just as well had fallen through a mine shaft considering the pain that followed. Not that I couldn't have managed (Beware: the male ego speaking here), but he was sure helpful when I wanted a pain reliever and couldn't drive to the drugstore.

And that same friend came forward when my car got stuck in a snowstorm one winter not to many years ago—and just when I was low on gas. I well remember our conversation through my cell phone.

"Hey, Slick," he greeted me with his patented chuckle. "Hope you're keeping warm and dry."

"Dry enough at the moment, but not particularly warm," I returned.

"Don't tell me your furnace conked out."

"It's not that, it's the car. It just as well have conked out. I can't budge it an inch. Reckon you can fire up that 4-wheel-drive pickup of yours and come give a poor unfortunate fellow a big lift out of a deep hole?"

While my body was freezing, I couldn't help appreciating that tug on the other end of his tow chain—and his warm heart.

He has never failed to be reliable and I thank God for him. I am a firm believer that if it came down to it, he would lay down his life for me. Now that's a true blue friend, and as I always say: "A true blue friend is a friend that keeps you from *being* blue."

I remember another time not long ago I had borrowed an old high school buddy's car and managed to place a ding on the front fender from a parking lot lamp post. It wasn't that serious, but it was definitely noticeable. When I returned the vehicle with sunken heart and sheepish grin, he wasn't particularly happy about it, but he surveyed the damage with a rub of the chin and calmly said to me, "It's not that bad. I have a friend who owns a body shop across the street from where I work who owes me a favor. He'll have it hammered out and like new in no time."

Who you know can certainly make a difference. A dentist who's a good friend may offer discounts on dental work. A carpenter who you befriended during that stint in the Army might come across with very inexpensive storm windows for your house. You could very well find some extra food in your cupboard thanks to a grocery store manager you've known half your life.

Not that it's a one-sided affair by any stretch. Once I came to the aid of my widower neighbor whose son lived 50 miles away. He had fallen from a ladder while attempting to trim a pecan tree and cracked a couple of ribs. I took him to the doctor and drove to the grocery store for him until he got better.

I've taken both friends and other neighbors to grocery stores when the need arose, helped them work on their cars, loaned them money (not too much), and even played baby-sitter a time or two. And, you know something, I'll be darned if it doesn't feel better than when *I* was being pulled out of a jam.

Unfortunately, I've found that's an easy fact to forget, hence the reason we should remind ourselves of it frequently by springing to the aid of our fellow man whenever the occasion arises. Why not? You'll find there is always someone willing to help *you*.

The whole thing might best be summed up by Ralph Waldo Emerson, who once said, "The only way to have a friend is to be one."

The point is: if the going gets rough in later years, and the tough aren't quite tough enough to endure well without help, friends are good medicine, whether one needs to get things off his chest or to get reassurance, or perhaps even to listen to advice. Personally, I am inclined to give advice—at just about every available opportunity, too, and more. (Why is it I sometimes get the impression I've overdone it?)

Strangers can quickly become friends as well. One time when I was out of work and my wife and I were beginning to get desperate, there was a knock at the front door. Already walking away were several children, one probably no more than 6, the other two, pre-teens or maybe even teenagers. But placed on the porch was several bags of groceries. Word of our plight had gotten around. They wouldn't say who they were, but that got us out of an immediate jam.

I was curious about the identity of those children who, it turned out, had been asked by their parents to carry out this deed on their behalf. Phyllis was likewise curious and some time later managed to tickle the grapevine in just the right places to get an answer. You know women.

But that was fortunate, indeed, because that gave us the opportunity to repay them with a nice spaghettis dinner, a few other tidbits and a dessert of jello (strawberry, I think). They may have been strangers, although they lived in our neighborhood, but wouldn't you more accurately label such strangers as "friends"?

And friends aren't just people who serve as a confidant or are around when you need them for an emergency or a difficult time. They are also there for what I like to call the "fish-tale-swapping" occasions—that is, to share the fun times. I have a friend named Calvin with which I used to go bowling every Friday night. The only hitch was that he beat me most of the time. But we both enjoyed the game and still had a good time. He was quite the bowler.

I remember on one occasion when Calvin was faced with the 6-7-8-10 split. One of the guys at the alley bet the "Old Master," as they sometimes called him, all the money he had in his pocket that wouldn't be able to pick it up. Calvin was one of those kind who was not bothered by pressure. If anything, he was driven by it. He proceeded to pick up his ball and calmly make his usual delivery—and he actually converted the spare!

Surprised as everyone else including me, the man who made the wager thought fast enough to tell Calvin, "I didn't say which pocket."

As the man twitched, Calvin shrugged it off. He was happy enough just to have accomplished the feat.

I strongly suspect the fellow's money pocket was far from full anyway, and I'm sure Calvin thought likewise. I also imagine the man was a shade more careful the next time he "placed a bet."

It has always been pleasant to have a partner not only for bowling, but for attending ball games, playing cards (although this might be something that some of you find wiser not to let your wife in on), and, yes, for fishing too (you know, to verify the size of that trout that might be used in a future tale).

I assure you, though, my fish stories are truthful. Really. On one occasion I had gone to a fishing barge with Asuka, a Japanese neighbor who had become a good friend. There were plenty of average-sized fish, with one exception—a big one that had become known as "Great Grand Daddy." I spent some time trying for it, but it never came near my line. I finally gave up and changed my bait. It wasn't long before Great Grand Daddy approached. But he turned his nose up to the worm on my hook and swam away in defiance. I wished I had stayed with my dough bait a little longer. I'm sure you'll agree that the story is perfectly truthful— and it should be since it's so believable.

Asuka and I never had much luck that day even on the smaller catches, but it turned out to be a good lesson in patience for me. And both of us had a lot of fun trying. We got to spend a great deal of time getting to know each other even better, as it was 90% gab and 10% action.

I also got to know Calvin a lot better when we thought we traveled to West Texas to attend a star party. If you are unfamiliar, a star party is a get-together of a group of people who are interested in astronomy who spend a week camped in the out-of-doors, staying up all night and observing the heavenly bodies with their optical aids. I was impressed with many of the larger telescopes (especially since I had brought along nothing more than a pair of binoculars and Calvin a 6-inch refractor). One kindly, long-bearded fellow gave us a peek through his 20-inch scope at the North American Nebula. Another guy let us see a few things in his 30-inch telescope. To our surprise, he told us his instrument was so powerful, he needed a filter when viewing the moon, or risk eye damage. Night was not the only time of activity. Once during the daylight hours we got to see the solar prominences and sunspots, complete with penumbras (the lighter shaded areas surrounding the sunspots). We learned the only way one could see the prominences was with a special device known as a hydrogen alpha filter. Ordinary solar filters would not work.

While we were there, Calvin and I also visited the temporary low-power FM station on the grounds established for the express purpose of keeping us informed with weather reports and other news of concern. It was nothing more than a man in a trailer who had been granted a license by the FCC to broadcast for one week. He informed us that it had been too much red tape to secure the license and he did not plan to repeat his performance when the star party assembled the next year. "For whatever it was worth, it was a once-in-a-lifetime experience," I told Calvin later and he concurred.

I was certainly glad I attended. That week was special—made even better because I met several new friends while I was there. A couple of them I still talk to on a semi-regular basis.

If you want to survive into the 80's, 90's or even beyond, I think friends are imperative. Hopefully, you have at least one good chum. If you aren't long on friends or want to meet new ones, be a joiner. Clubs, church groups and the like can be of help. Also, try www.seniorpeoplemeet.com to meet seniors in your area.

You can even make new acquaintances via the internet through newsgroups and become pen pals for life. (I remember the time a high school mate who lived on my street established a number of pen pals, some even in foreign countries. And that was during the era of snail mail. They kept each other up with the latest, discussed their experiences, and even sent presents to each other.)

If you are looking for an old friend, check www.facebook.com. As the website says, "Connect and share with the people in your life."

Other websites include: My Space (www.myspace.com), Twitter (www.twitter.com) and LinkedIn (www.linkedin.com).

You can also check www.mylife.com. Not only will you have a chance to locate a long lost buddy, but you can even see who might be searching for you!

CHAPTER 7:

SPORTS: BEING PART OF THE ACTION

I'm talking exercise here. This doesn't mean watching another Mets game on TV, or giving your fingers a workout in a card game, but active participation that gives muscles a challenge—yet something that can be fun exercise. So things like skiing and hand ball are out of reason, as is most likely tennis. But how about golf? Or

bowling? Or badminton? Or ping-pong? Even shuffleboard or croquette keeps you in reasonable motion. If nothing more, you can toss the ball around with the grand kids or their children. Any sport such as these is acceptable as long as it is approved by your doctor.

I've tried many of them during my lifetime with special fondness of the games of catch with my grandson. It always afforded me the opportunity to be in his company while I got needed exercise. And in all those times, we only cracked—well smashed—one window. (I hate to 'fess up to whose fault that was, so I won't.)

I became especially fond of bowling in my youthful days and it wasn't long before I owned by own ball—one of those with silver specks. I was on a number of leagues throughout the years. Once we (a church group) were awarded for being the second place team. Of course, I still have the trophy I received, prominently displayed on the mantle. I was no hot bowler, but I do remember those particularly good games, such as the time I started out the first three frames with a turkey (three strikes in a row, if you're not familiar), or the game in which I finally broke 200.

There were some big achievements at the alleys that I frequented. In one game a league bowler was awarded for picking up the 7-10 split, the envy of any professional. I only heard about this later, but wish I had been there to see it. Then there was the time a bowler was on a big roll and had accumulated strikes through the first 9 frames. Everybody held his breath on the 10th, but it was not enough. He only got 8 pins—and then left an open frame. My heart really went out to the guy. It would have been fun to witness a perfect game by an amateur.

Oh, but if only one of those feats had been mine! I could only dream about becoming an exceptional bowler and did it through the pros. I'd watch the bowling tours on TV quite often and envy the abilities of such greats as Don Carter.

Although fond of the wide open spaces and fresh air, I never went in as much for golf. It always seemed more frustrating to me. And I was never any better golfer than I was a bowler. Whenever I played, the birdies took flight and I struggled to make par.

But once, I witnessed a hole in one. The tall-faced, stout-legged fellow that drove it home, was a friend of a friend, so I didn't know him, but he didn't appeared to be more than a fair golfer. As it was he only beat me by a few strokes. (That should tell you something.) It was unbelievable. The ball hit the green and rolled forward straight for the cup as if it had eyes—and it was a noticeably breezy day. (Some guys have all the luck.)

I found it better to just limit myself to miniature golf. I figured it was the only way I held a chance of sinking a hole in one myself and, yes, I can boast to having several. I even won a free game once in Estes Park, Colorado when I was 12 years old.

I used to watch miniature golf tournaments on TV whenever I wanted to see lots of holes in one. I couldn't help but marvel over and envy those professionals who participated. I still remember the announcer's voice as it rang out on so many of the first putts: "It's up, over and into the cup."

Probably the reason I have developed such a warm place in my heart for miniature golf is because it is another game that's excellent for playing with the kids. I have not known a single young person who didn't like it. On a number of occasions, I invited my grandchildren along for a game and then we went and bought snow cones afterward.

Croquette is another game suited for playing with the youngsters. We've had several family parties in which the croquette set came out, often at the insistence of one of the kids. And, of course, with my help, one of them always managed to win. I suppose that beats putting yourself under pressure to achieve a 250 bowling score.

I've toyed with the idea of taking up ping pong one of these fine days. I can always find a partner, but I very much fear I wouldn't be any better at it than I have been with bowling or golf. So be it, as long as it's fun exercise I might just break down and give it a whirl.

CHAPTER 8:

EXERCISE: MAKING A HIT WITH YOUR BODY BY KEEPING FIT

If you're not inclined toward participating sports (Is that possible for the male species?), there's always other means of exercise. Exercise is excellent for enhancing and maintaining physical fitness—as long as it involves more than just flexing your fingers in a card game. It can contribute positively to maintaining a healthy weight, healthy bone density, muscle strength, and joint mobility. In addition, it promotes physiological well-being, strengthens the immune system, and reduces surgical risks.

Walking is probably the most popular example. It's worthwhile exercise as long as you snub the mid-summer sun and the winter frost. Walking falls under the category of aerobic exercise. Aerobic exercise helps increase cardiovascular endurance. In addition, according to a 2008 review of cognitive enrichment therapies (strategies to retard or reverse cognitive decline), physical activity such as aerobic exercise increases the older adult's cognitive function. Other examples are cycling, swimming, rowing and skipping rope.

I prefer to walk. I've seen a number of others who are evidently of the same opinion, some taking a radio walkman along with them. But I always considered that a burden. The only thing I've ever taken along with me is one of several dogs I've own during my lifetime. When I'm walking, I would rather allow my mind to unwind and wonder, not listen to reports on how much inflation has risen or what bill congress is considering next. And I find a constitutional to be quite stimulating. So I give my muscles a workout while I rest my brain on an almost daily basis. I cover the block several times during these sessions and probably do somewhat more than a mile. If conditions are not favorable, I use a nearby shopping mall. But

I'd rather be on the street because I enjoy the fresh air. And I do it in the morning before the pollution begins to build and add staleness to the environment.

Often, I've killed the proverbial two birds with one stone and hiked down to the store a quarter of a mile away to grab a loaf of bread or some other item my wife forgot to pick up the day before. (It feels good to save gasoline.) I even made the trip a couple of times and brought back the wrong item. Somehow we survived it.

One time I made myself useful and helped a repairman lift an air conditioning unit over a fence. Another time I came home with a dog—not mine—who was adorned with tags. The charcoal gray pooch of a breed I don't remember had taken an immediate liking to me and followed me home. I called the number posted on the tags and informed the owner who came soon after to claim her animal. She was a tall, dark woman, who was very appreciative, and insisted on giving me a 5-dollar reward.

I've grown so accustomed to walking that it has become second nature to me when I want to conduct business at the neighborhood shopping center. Not only is there a grocery store, but our bank, a drugstore and a library. One time, however, I got lazy and took the car. There were a couple of library books I wanted to return that would have been overdue the next day. I dropped them in the chute and took the time while I was there to browse. Not finding anything else that inspired me to check out, I walked casually out the door and started down the street. I was into the next block before it dawned on me I had forgotten the car!

Walking is usually a pleasant affair, but sometimes I've run into trouble. Once a dog took a good-sized nip at my leg. It felt like a vice had closed over it. Fortunately there was nothing to worry about. My pants were thick and the dog was old, his teeth dull. He didn't even break the skin.

Another time I got caught in a downpour and got soaked through and through. Naturally, the barrage began when I was on the far side of the block. I was warned that rain was in the forecast and the sky was certainly leaden enough, but I was determined to get in at least one round. I had skipped several days. Phyllis was convinced that I was going to catch cold, but I fooled her and didn't.

I've considered cycling, but then I would have to invest in a bicycle and that costs money. (As you may conclude, I'm a penny-pincher.) But if you have a bicycle or want to buy one, don't let me stop you. At least you can cover a lot more ground.

I'd be more inclined to take up swimming, at least on a semi-regular basis (like, say, summertime only), but I hate the smell of chlorine. Besides, my swim trunks no longer fit and I'm not about to buy any more of those. So as far as contact with water is concerned, I'll just stick to a hot tub or the shower.

At any rate, don't be afraid to take on any exercise your doctor approves in your particular situation. It will help you to keep active and, who knows, you may even find yourself creaking a little less. But no matter which kind you choose, don't overdo it. As my grandfather once discovered in the Army, "You can get your second wind, but there ain't no *third* wind."

CHAPTER 9:

TRAVELING IN STYLE —OR ANY WAY YOU LIKE

There's something refreshing about geographically removing yourself from your everyday surroundings. In my younger days, that fact was obvious. I could hardly wait until vacation time came around and I could get away from my job for a couple of weeks. The farther away I went, the better.

When you get older, however, such is not as noticeable—at least not with me. I kind of forget I need a change from the usual and I get stale long before I realize it. I assume it's because I'm retired and don't have anything in the way of regular labor I am seeking to get away from.

Therefore, I caution you: Don't hesitate to travel when the opportunity avails itself. There is lots to see in this great country, not to mention abroad. And grumpiness doesn't survive well in the midst of a vacation. I can't remember a single trip I took in which I was the least bit out of sorts.

I've been to every corner of the country and seen the Golden Gate Bridge, Yellowstone Park, the Grand Canyon, the St. Louis archway, the Royal Gorge, Pike's Peak, Hollywood, the redwood forest, the French Quarter, Carlsbad Caverns, Mount Rushmore, Four Corners, Edmonton Mall, Epcot Center, the Statue of Liberty, Disneyland—and even the old London Bridge in Lake Havasu City, Arizona. I've also ventured out of the country far enough to see Mexico, Canada and Jamaica.

I never thought much of flying in your own "backyard." Oh, you get there fast enough, but you miss so much along the way. So we have usually opted for motor trips when traveling in the United States. I remember one time we started out for I don't remember where in our almost new Ford Granada and on a whim broke our itinerary and wound up over the border and in Winnipeg, Manitoba. It was a lot of fun to just lose ourselves for a while. I was impressed with the city's numerous wide boulevards and spacious parks. I couldn't help wondering, though, what it would be like in the debt of winter.

I remember when visiting Hollywood and seeing the set where the TV series "The Incredible Hulk" was being filmed. Unfortunately, the star Bill Bixby was not there that day. That was disappointing, but there was so much more to see and I soon forgot about that one little ripple by the time we got to Grauman's Chinese Theater.

While we were in Hollywood, we got tickets to sit in on one of the game shows while they were filming it. I don't remember the name of the program. It wasn't one of the popular ones, unfortunately, and was soon cancelled. But it was a hoot to be part of the studio audience and pull for the contestants to win.

Carlsbad Caverns became my first experience in a cave. I had been warned to take heavy clothing and wished I had brought along a thicker jacket. It was hard to believe how cold one can get in the middle of the summer just because you are a little ways underground. That was the only time I ever grew tired of walking down. Not to complain. The cave formations were awesome.

Then there was the time in Phoenix, Arizona we decided to walk from the motel to a nearby Chinese restaurant for dinner. "A few blocks isn't so far," you might say, yet we made it a daring day. The temperature was hovering near 122! But we were only 59 then (well, O. K., 60). I wouldn't do it again *now* and don't recommend it for anyone else.

When I was in Yellowstone, sitting on a nearby bench, I marveled over Old Faithful, respecting nature probably more than I ever had. I couldn't resist the temptation to time that ancient geyser with my watch several times, but of course, I failed to catch it in error.

We enjoyed walking trails in Colorado. There were some beautiful cascades, wildflowers and breathtaking views from the near distance. All went well until my wife felt the strain in one of her leg muscles. The kids expressed an interest in continuing, but we were forced to call a halt and switch our activity to horseback riding. I have often hoped to get back there and try some of the other trails. Perhaps next year we'll make it so.

On our first visit to San Francisco, we enjoyed sipping oolong tea and eating a fish dinner while watching the Pacific at our doorstep. It was almost exactly on the anniversary of the great earthquake.

And there was that cool, cloudy day at Four Corners. What a major feat it seemed to travel from state to state within seconds and to occupy 4 states of this great nation all at once.

Memories, oh, what memories—and some of them quite novel! On one of our trips to the Rocky Mountains, we actually found ourselves looking down upon a rainbow. Got a good shot of it too. (Remember the old Brownie movie cameras?) On another trip somewhere in Colorado, we were handed the privilege of feeding bread to a deer that was bold enough or hungry enough to come forward. And, then, there was that total solar eclipse we witnessed the time we were in Atlanta. The weather people later reported that the event dropped the temperature 6 degrees.

There were other memories in the form of challenging surprises, like the time we barely slipped into Santa Fe, New Mexico with a malfunctioning distributor (a lesson for keeping one's automobile in good condition). There, we were rescued by a stooped over mechanic who turned out to be most accommodating. He pushed us ahead of two other customers so we could be on our way. Four hours later, we had a smooth-running engine once more.

We also experienced more than a few anxious moments the time we got delayed because of an April snowfall in West Texas. The rare phenomenon had completely fooled the weather bureau and we began to wonder if we were going to make it without snow chains, which we didn't have at the time because we never fathomed that we would need such a thing during a Texas spring. Fortunately, the highway never got too slick. The next day it cleared up and was warm and beautiful for the rest of our trip.

And what a sobering experience it was when I encountered a particularly jovial man with a moon face seated at an outside table in Jamaica. We had quite a conversation, although he did most of the talking, carrying an air that all was right with the world and he was glad to be a part of it. It was a bright day (and I'm not particularly observant, anyway) and I thought nothing about the sunglasses he was wearing until he rose to make his departure whereupon I discovered he was also in possession of a cain—an instrument he wielded in the fashion that only the sightless would! I enjoyed my stay, but it now held a special new meaning and I was immensely grateful for the ability to take pleasure in my surroundings on a visual level.

Indeed, fun it has always been to travel—even more so when you share it with the grandchildren, or if you're lucky enough, with great grandchildren—even when you have to supply a frequent answer for the famous line, "Are we there yet?"

Watching their eyes light up while feeding the chipmunks or hearing their giggles when doing the circuit at an amusement can be as much a thrill as the whole trip. In fact, our two grandchildren were present when we fed the deer.

And there's nothing like the crisp mountain air of Colorado and the partaking of mountain water when you've been sweltering in the heat of summer; or the tranquility of a small Connecticut town when you've been battling traffic in the big city; sinking your bare feet into warm beach sand after enduring an exceptionally cold winter; or biting into those special fresh pastries, the flavor of which only the French Quarter seems able to provide. Even reading a different newspaper, listening to a different radio station, or watching a different TV channel can add spice to the whole thing. Once when we were in Kansas City, I got to see "Dennis the Menace", a series that hadn't aired in our area for ages. (That was before the advent of satellite dishes, VCRs and DVRs.)

And, of course, you don't have to stop with the United States or the North American continuant for that matter. Get out and see the rest of the world. Flying is acceptable then (as long as you don't get too impetuous and try for Mars). Take a flight to Europe, Australia or the Orient. If you're not flight inclined, you might consider a cruise.

Now that the Iron Curtain has long since been lifted, there is no better time. Know what it's like to take in the Rhine River, to see Red Square in person, to examine the green meadows of Austria, or to look up at the Eiffel Tower—if not look down *from* it (just don't jump). And you can also appreciate the majesty of the Swiss Alps, get a first-hand look at the great wall of China, stroll the beaches of Australia, bow your head in the Holy Land, and a lot more.

The website www.traveling.com offers vacation packages, and there you can search for hotels and make reservations. Check www.travelocity.com to book travel for less, with specials on cheap airline tickets, hotels, cruises and car rentals. Also look up the vacation spots of your choice on the internet. You can garner a wealth of information at numerous websites.

CHAPTER 10:

PETS

There's nothing like a pet for us older folks. Lot's of senior couples enjoy them, but if you are a widower or divorced—or a well-established bachelor—and live alone, they can be even more important, as they not only offer amusement and help pass otherwise hollow hours, but they readily alleviate loneliness. I wouldn't recommend anything offbeat such as a snake. And no fair picking on horses or parrots (unless you already own one). They would probably out live you by a wide margin. But dogs, cats and parakeets are good bets.

I was always partial to the canine breed, as it seems dogs are easier to take care of than cats or birds. One dog I owned was nothing short of phenomenal. He was a pure black, white and brown mutt named Snookers who had developed an extensive vocabulary—including verbs as well as nouns. Just some on the list were: give, visitor, go present (as in gift), want, sack, frisbee, ball, walk, chair, toy, bone, inside, outside, mail, trash, that's all, move, leash, tail, play, apple, peanuts, water, bowl and eat. It's a shame I couldn't have taught him how to diagram a sentence!

Snookers knew every trick in the book. And he not only responded to verbal commands, but would answer to hand gestures as well. You could tell him to come, sit, lay down, roll over, twirl, crawl, bark, wave, wag, go to bed, you name it.

Not only did he know the tricks I taught him, but he had some "up his sleeve" as well. He was the kind of dog who would never run off, so you could trust him to go unleashed when you were walking him (O. K. as long as the dog catcher wasn't around). He was well aware that I didn't want him eating food out of garbage cans or off the street. I was particular about what I fed him. But he was a real schemer and would play innocent. On certain occasions I would notice him lagging behind me and every time I would look back, he would squat as if to be relieving himself. That told me he was in the midst of an investigation to size the area up for an extra meal. Sometimes he was tired after one time around the block, other times he wanted to go around again. (I've always done three laps.) Quite often, when he expressed a desire to continue the constitutional with me, it meant he had spotted something of sizeable proportion somewhere along the way and was biding his time, waiting to make the second chance count. On one occasion, lagging even farther behind me on the second circuit, it turned out to be a whole hamburger patty, complete with ants crawling over it, resting near the curb three-quarters of the way around. I was ready for him, although he managed to get a few bites of it before I could put a stop to his extracurricular activity. As it was, there is no telling how many morsels he lapped up over time that I didn't know about and he didn't want me knowing about, but for a dog to maintain that kind of discipline in an attempt to fool me was astounding.

Snookers was a real pal, though. He was with me when I took out the garbage, when I went for the mail, and when I was working in the yard. And he enjoyed being a comedian. He would make those silly little moves that would induce a smile, if not laughter, in the family. He had spirit, too, and would "play games" with you. If you were too busy to play ball at the time he wanted, he would make sure to refuse you with a sulk the next time you volunteered your cooperation—even if it was only minutes later—and even though it was obvious he still wanted to play.

A few times I took him to the park and we played with a Frisbee. I'll never forget his expression the first time we did this and I had finally told him it was time to go. I looked into his eyes and it was as if they were saying, "Do we have to go now? Isn't there something even more fun you can do with me?"

Once while we were walking, we got caught in a big downpour. That was where Snooker's loyalty hit its limit. He darted away from me and ran back to the house, seeking shelter on the front porch. He was sticking his neck out as far as he could without getting any wetter, watching diligently as I rounded the corner of the block, soaked to the skin. Did I hold it against him? Not by any stretch!

Once Snookers displayed his remarkable character in a moment I will never forget. I had placed a hamburger on the coffee table in the living room so I could eat while I was watching a big ball game. After only a few bites, I had to step out to the bathroom. When I returned, he was reared up against the tray with wistful eyes, his mouth touching the hamburger, but without having consumed one crumb. He won my heart and got the burger anyway. I figured he earned it after maintaining that kind of discipline.

Needless to say, Snookers was popular with the family and deeply loved. Everyone would regularly go around praising Snookers with the line, "You're a good dog" in a high baby-talk voice. Pretty soon, a non-human member of the family picked up on it and often bubbled forth with the same line—not the dog, but a parakeet named Peppy that we owned at the time—although I wouldn't have been surprised to have heard it from Snookers himself.

Snookers possessed another interesting characteristic. He would always greet visitors not only with a full tail wag, but with a smile. His lip would curl slightly on one side just enough to show his teeth. That was the thing that inspired us to nickname him "The Human Dog."

I owned another dog named Shadow who possessed a peculiar habit. You always knew when something didn't set well with her because she always displayed her protest by ruffling the bath mats. Her only other downfall was that she developed a phobia for bad weather in later years and had to be reassured whenever it began to rain. At least she wasn't afraid of her *shadow*.

When she was not far past puppyhood, we once let her inside before we realized her paws were caked with mud from a rain. My wife stopped her at the door and ordered her to lay downright there, demanding that she "clean off those feet" before she was permitted access to the rest of the house. Sure enough, the dog complied by biting off every bit of debris and depositing it in a neat little pile beside her. No matter how bad conditions got after that, she never repeated the incident.

Whenever the grandchildren came to visit, she would get so excited, it almost seemed the *dog* was wagging the *tail*. She would shake so violently from excitement at the prospect of gaining extra playmates, I almost expected her to come apart any minute.

She would react the same way on two other occasions. When you told her it was time for supper and when you offered to give her a massage. I do believe she actually loved the back rubs more than she did eating. As soon as I would start to dig in, her mouth would get wide with delight and when it was over (all too soon as far as she was concerned, I'm sure), she would breath a large-sized sigh and plop down in one of her favorite corners.

My next door neighbor owned a dog who all too often whined for seemingly no reason, as if pleading for something—he didn't know what. He once told me, "I got the impression the animal wanted me and my family to turn into dogs to play with him."

Every dog I owned was treated well. They had nice soft beds with a pillow, lots of extra snacks (more than they should have had) in addition to regular meals, and one giant "dog" house, which they willingly shared with us. I'm sure they all figured in their canine way that *man* is *dog's* best friend.

Off course, dogs aren't the only pets available. Consider a cat if your preference leans toward the feline nature. Possessing a grace and agility all their own, these lovable creatures never grow very large and are a pleasure to feed and play with. Their appetites aren't ferocious either. And cats are quiet creatures as opposed to the average dog, in addition to being just as cute. They have good long lives (as long as you keep them *away* from certain dogs, not to mention speeding automobiles).

Although they usually have a shy personality (except with mice), there are exceptions. I remember one cat, a large white one, who began striding along with me on the street one day as if it *was* a dog. I'm sure its size gave it a big feeling od security. One friend across town owned a cat that he said would sometimes prissily stride about with a ball of yarn as if she herself had manufactured it. She had a favorite spot on a windowsill where she would watch the children come home from school everyday. (I don't know what she did on weekends and holidays.) Once she almost jumped through the screen when a mockingbird landed on the outside of it.

I never had the pleasure of owning a cat, but there were a number of fowl in my life in the form of parakeets. We owned a dark blue one (the one we called Peppy), a light blue one named Chipper (who was very feisty), and a yellow one who I forgot the name of—and who died prematurely from a disease we never identified.

Peppy would eat anything, including seed. I'd sometimes offer him a bite of buttered biscuit for breakfast, or a piece of a French fry during lunch, or maybe a nibble of fruit at dinner. He loved it all and sang with delight.

I couldn't say the same for Chipper, however. This bird made it difficult for you to feed at all because he would often squawk and bite at you when you were placing the seed tray in the cage. And he certainly was not going the consume anything but seed. That just goes to show you the wide variety of personalities one can find in animals. But we overlooked his unruliness and loved him (or was it her) just the same.

And I will never forget the school teacher who lived across the alley from where I lived as a child who owned a large collection of parakeets of every color that she kept in her backyard in an outside cage the size of small storage room. She was the talk of the neighborhood.

If none of the afore mentioned pets catch your fancy, there's another possibility: an aquarium. A tank full of fish can be interesting as well as convey an air of tranquility.

I owned a large aquarium at one point during my bachelor days, containing angel fish, cat fish, a silver dollar fish, guppies, a beta, and tetras. The other fish eventually ate the little tetras, which I couldn't resist adding to the tank, despite a warning that this could happen. Things went well (at least with the other fish) until I was away on a winter weekend trip and the power failed, turning off not only the heat in the house, but the fish tank heater as well. When I returned to an icy house (the temperature standing at 10 degrees outside), they were all dead and I gave up on the whole deal, although I had at one time considered adding a salt water tank.

But the aquarium was a lot of fun. The fish all began to swim joyfully when I would return home form work everyday, knowing their master was about to feed them. (Too bad I couldn't get them to smile like Snookers.) I fed them the regular fish food and occasionally switched off, giving them a treat of brine shrimp. I'm sure owning a salt water tank would have been just as much fun as the fresh water one, and both would have undoubtedly proven even more interesting.

If you don't own an aquarium, and like the idea, by all means consider purchasing one. If you don't desire anything quite that elaborate, opt for a bowl of goldfish.

But whether it's fish, a dog or whatever, I heartily recommend a pet, especially if you live alone. More times than I could ever count pets have distracted me from my worries. And I can never recall a time that I was grumpy while I was feeding or playing with, or just observing one of them.

CHAPTER 11:

HOBBIES: THE FUN SIDE OF LIFE

I've learned that when I get really riled, I can get rid of a lot of excess steam by resorting to my hobbies. I have an extensive collection of old time radio shows and classic TV series. I can always soothe myself with episodes of *The Shadow* or an installment or two of *The Honeymooners*. I own 8-tracks, cassettes, reel-to-reel tapes, video tapes, and DVDs. But now I have the convenience of enjoying the programs through a computer. In fact, my entire collection of old radio shows now reside on a single hard drive.

I used to trade these programs to several others who had collections of their own via snail mail. First it was reel tape for radio shows and later video tape for TV shows and movies. I'd dub off the selections they wanted and send the copies to them and they would do likewise with me. It was fun waiting for the mail everyday, anticipating the arrival of the next tape. Now you can upload and download all the shows you want on a computer thanks to newsgroups.

I also have a collection of record albums. It's nice to have access to music such as done by Lawrence Welk, Ray Conniff, Tony Bennett, and many other old favorites. As with the radio programs, I have them all digitized on a hard drive.

Also, I love to write. I've been at it since my age was measured in single digits. For years I'd pull out pen and paper and have a go at another short story. The only thing that has changed is that I now punch letters on a keyboard and make them visible on a computer monitor. It's good therapy and keeps my mind sharp.

Then there's gardening. I usually grow something most every season, even if it's just a few tomatoes. In most cases, although I can't say I have a green thumb, the effort is worth what I get out of it. One year I could do no wrong with squash and there were several servings of it for the family and neighbors, despite the fact that some of it got snitched by passersby. (It was the last time I planted that close to the fence.) Another year, I had good luck with cantaloupe. One time, however, the usual reliable green bean plants failed to break ground for a suspiciously long interval and I investigated by digging up some of the seeds. They had failed to germinate and were covered with some kind of fungus. I never did figure out how that happened. It makes one take pity on farmers who have to rely on their crops for survival.

Occasionally, I've even shared in someone else's hobby, such as the time I made a boat trip to the lake with a neighbor who was a fanatic about water travel. It was not without adventure, however, as we wound up catching the engine propellers on something beneath the surface of a shallow stretch of water. The engine died and we were unable to fire it back up again. We had to use the trolling motor to get back to shore. Fortunately we weren't too far out. My neighbor blamed the depth gage, despite the fact neither one of us were watching it at the moment. He finally sold the boat to someone who we later found out neglected to run the motor in a bucket of water while he tested it in his driveway and was faced with a major repair job.

If you don't have a hobby and are interested, here is just a small suggestion list:

Photography	Genealogy
Astronomy	Chess
Electronics	Magic Tricks
Woodworking	Painting
Ham Radio	Music
Bird Watching	Wine making
Boating	Writing
Traveling	Collecting
Gardening	

This last category, collecting, includes much more than just what's related to stamps or coins, but anything imaginable: baseball trading cards, record albums, books, classic magazines, bottle caps, butterflies, business cards, guns, photographs, baseball caps, ice hockey pucks, keys, ticket stubs, clocks, calendars, post cards, letterheads, autographs, old time radio shows, and DVDs to name only a few.

I'm certainly one for collecting. Tapes and records aren't the only thing I've accumulated over the years. You might say I collect collections. Anything part of a series has always fascinated me. Most of it is considered junk by my wife, of course. But that's one thing women don't understand, unless it concerns amassing a sizeable wardrobe.

You should see my collection of view master slides, modest as it is, that I've owned since I was a little boy, faded, but still viewable. I have a series on travel covering many countries of the world: Venezuela, Yugoslavia, Burma, Portugal, Spain, Switzerland, Brazil, India, to name but a few. Then there's *Carlsbad Caverns, Rocky Mountain National Park, and the Royal Gorge*. Other slides include: *Aesops Fables, Robinson Crusoe, Gulliver's Travels, 2,000 Leagues Under the Sea, Man on the Moon*, and several TV series. It's most interesting to view scenes from an episode of *Voyage to the Bottom of the Sea* or *Mission: Impossible* in 3-D.

Then I have my trading cards, you know, those kind you used to get with bubble gum. There are ones on baseball, football, and other sports as well as those related to monsters and spooks, outer space, the Civil War, etc.

And while I'm good and wound up about it, I don't want to forget my coin collection. There are lots of foreign ones, including one with a hole in the middle (from India, I think), some I received from my aunt and uncle that they procured from the Mardi Gras in New Orleans (which are big, colorful, and light weight—and not legal tender), and even one octagon-shaped coin I got somewhere in Canada redeemable for $1.00 (1 astron) at any store or bank on the moon until 12-31-1969! And I own a slew of old keys and business cards. I'll leave my book collection to your imagination. I'm sure I can find more items lying around I forgotten about, but at this point I'd better surrender.

It's interesting the things that hold fascination for the male human being. My father used to collect newspaper write-ups of all the local baseball games. I know someone who collects Disney memorabilia. I've heard of one person who adores old record players, including the ones that play those ancient cylindrical-shaped records. And I was once told about a gentleman that holds a deep intrigue for buses, who bought one—and only one—and fixed it up to show off. Then there's the classic car buff, who may be lucky enough to own several vehicles (I might just as well make a go for yachts), and those who hold dear to anything about World War II, the Civil War, auto racing, trains, aircraft, or any number of other such things.

My pastimes are not restricted to collections. Sometimes, if I'm not writing, I just relax at the park with my binoculars and take in some bird watching. I've also brought along my binoculars on trips and spotted birds that I wouldn't likely spot at home. Once I saw a cluster of goldfinch that would knock your eyes out. I've also identified blue jays, cardinals, robins, mockingbirds, wild parrots, and waxwings. I love the markings of the waxwing, which looks as though it had dipped the tip of its tail into a can of yellow paint, as bright as the color of the goldfinch.

Many times I've turned my binoculars skyward and seen the 4 largest moons of Jupiter, the rings of Saturn, comets, meteor showers, lunar eclipses and the like. When conditions were just right, I was privileged to see the planet Venus in the daytime! Once I spotted a bright "star" that shouldn't have been where it was and began to think I had spotted a genuine UFO. The binoculars, however, quickly dispelled the idea when it brought into view a weather balloon.

You can even combine one of several hobbies into a nice, neat package. My friend Calvin loves photography as much as he does astronomy. Not content to just look into his telescope, he attached a camera to it and now takes celestial photos. He has some beautiful pictures of the galaxies, the planets, and solar prominences.

Some hobbies can even make you money. I found that out when I sold my first short story. I also threw out some ads and sold radio shows for a while, but I gave that up because I was spending all the proceeds on tape to trade more shows and it was actually more fun just to get the programs in the mail rather than checks.

I strongly suggest every man have a hobby—at least every *grumpy* man. Whether it's a collection of whatever catches your fancy, or woodworking, writing, traveling, reading, or making music, it's sure to distract you from grumpiness.

CHAPTER 12:

ELECTRONIC PARAPHERNALIA

Hobbies often involve electronic toys but I thought it deserved a chapter all its own. I do believe men love electronic equipment as much as women adore dresses—probably *more* if you get right down to it. I always did have a liking for turning knobs and punching buttons. I guess it helps one to feel in command. When I was a boy I did it with an electronics kit I got for my birthday, activating buzzers, bells, blinking colored lights and little electric motors. Of course, such toys become more sophisticated as we grow older.

I can't speak for every old-timer, but I know how fun it was when I invested in a good shortwave radio. I listened to stations such as the Voice of America; AFRTS (Armed Forces Radio and Television Service), Radio Canada International; the BBC; and HCJB in Quito, Equador. I got different slants on world news and heard lots of ball games. I also received exotic music from stations I couldn't identify. One time during unusual atmospheric conditions, I actually received the audio portion from both a British and a French TV station. (This was long before communication satellites were in orbit to relay signals and I considered it quite a stoke of luck.) I don't speak French, but I did identify the English station as BBC-1. I wrote to them and they sent me a QSL card, verifying that I did indeed receive their programming. Owning a shortwave radio was a considerable upgrade from the days in my youth when I was playing with a crystal radio set that I had put together with one station to listen to—and that with a single headphone I had to hold to my ear.

Then there was the time when I graduated from a monaural table radio (you remember, the ones with vacuum tubes) to a stereo radio/amplifier. I could begin to appreciate the richer sound and added depth that music had to offer. Likewise, my first stereo tape deck was a special pleasure. Then I could enjoy the full benefit of my music collection. Who needed a monaural tape recorder anymore?

And it became a monumental moment in my life when I advanced from a black and white to a color television set. *Bonanza* never looked better. In fact, I became so enthusiastic that I had erected a 40-foot tower to make certain I got the best reception possible. My picture seemed incredibly sharp at the time, but my opinion has changed since the introduction of digital signals and High Definition. (One of these days I going to spring for a wide-screen TV.)

That was nothing compared to the time I procured my first VCR. It was convenient to come home from work and see a movie or other program that had run earlier that afternoon, but I couldn't resist the temptation to keep just about everything after I recorded it. It was limiting at first with VHS tapes running over $20,00 a piece, but I was delighted when the price began to drop. And I was grateful later that I had chosen VHS over the now defunct Betamax.

Then came the computer era. I'll admit I hesitated at first on this matter. Owning such a device seemed imposing beyond belief. I didn't really need a computer anyway, did I? As you may guess, I finally gave in one spring afternoon and made my purchase. Now I wonder how I ever got along without one.

My computer is not just fun to play with, it has become an essential piece of equipment for me. I wonder how I ever survived my early writing activities with nothing more than an ordinary typewriter and carbon paper—and, of course, an eraser. I no longer have to worry about correcting mistakes the hard way, or starting over a half dozen times and filling my waste basket with balls of paper. And there are no more typewriter ribbons to change. Now I can enjoy the ability to switch sentences or entire paragraphs around with a few clicks. What's really beautiful is that you don't necessarily have to print out what you write when it's possible to attach it to an E-mail and sent it to a publisher or anyone else you like—or simply post it on a webpage, just as you can photos and home movies.

But a computer has developed into something far more than just a glorified typewriter. It is now a personal post office. I can send E-mail to my family and friends, as well as receive it from them. It took some doing to break the habit of snail mail after years of knowing nothing else, but I eventually succeeded. Now rather than licking another stamp and making yet another trip to the post office, and then waiting days and days for a response, I can receive a return reply as soon as the receiving party has checked their E-mail and sent a message of their own!

I also own as electronic photo album. My hard drive is loaded with pictures of trips I've made, not to mention family, friends and pets. Now that I use a digital camera (another fun electronic toy), I can export photographs from it straight to the computer. And I no longer face the expense and the wait to have film developed. There are also many photographs taken years ago on a shelf in my closet that I have yet to scan, but one of these days I hope to do so.

In addition, I use the computer as a radio. There's lots of good music streaming on the web and I like to pull in the different stations and listen. Likewise, I have, in effect, turned my computer into a television set by playing DVDs.

The computer is also a library and a bookstore to me. I can find virtually any information I am looking for and order books as well as other items. I've forgotten all about my set of bicentennial edition encyclopedias.

Often, it is fun to just search the web. I've seen pictures of tourist sites in other countries, found information about movie stars that I was curious about, and even garnered instruction on how to clean my computer.

I've also used the internet to diagnose computer problems. I found out that there are times it is best to reformat the hard drive when the speed of its operation slows to the point of annoyance. And even more important, I have learned that above all else, you should always, but always, make it a habit to back up your data!

Computer peripherals, such as printers, make things even more fun. I sometimes use my printer to print information I've found on the internet that interests me or that is useful to keep for reference. But what I like to do most is to get really fancy and print pictures I have stored in my computer on good quality photo paper. I can then send them to people who don't own a computer. What's so wonderful is that they look just as good as the original snapshot.

Printers are good up to a point for me, but a scanner I've found to be even more useful. I've not only scanned photos (at least the most important ones so far), but a lot of my baseball cards. (One of these days I'm going to finish that project too.) Also on my scanning list just for the fun of it are business cards, postcards and letterheads. I have also scanned receipts and other business documents of which I've needed to keep copies. I have a folder on my hard drive for each category.

Of course, anything I put into the computer I always back up as soon as I can. It's easy now that I have an 8-gigabite flash drive that plugs into one of my USB ports. (I gave up on the old-fashioned method of making discs.) Flash drives are the greatest invention since the wheel. They're fast and very portable. You can take one with you in your pocket or on a key chain and share its content with a friend on his computer.

I wonder how anyone could keep up in today's fast-paced society without a computer. They've become as useful as a cell phone. If you don't have one, you don't know what you'rre missing. In fact, I must insist that you invest in a computer without delay. If you fail to comply, I'm going to look you up, come over and administer 10 lashes with a piece of my fishing line.

The same thing goes for a cell phone. The only difference is that I don't look at mine as a toy as I often do my computer, but I consider it a great convenience—if not a real lifesaver. Once I had just gotten down to the grocery store to pick up a few items for the little woman and had gone off without the list. All I had to do was march back out to the parking lot, grab the cell phone, and call her. Another time, again while I was grocery shopping, I couldn't find the kind of pickles she wanted and had to ask her what her second preference was. As it turned out, the brand I finally came away with tasted better than what we had been buying.

Cell phones certainly help you keep in touch no matter where you are, be it a block from the house or all the way across the nation. Phyllis was only a few finger punches away when I had to call her after a basketball game I was attending went into overtime. Then she knew I was all right and would have no need to fret when I didn't show up at the expected time. It not only saved *her* from worry, but *me* from worry about *her* worrying, as she all too often does.

It's always reassuring to have a cell phone near you "just in case." It becomes a sheer necessity when a crisis arises. Someone I know told me that a cell phone became a life saver to a neighbor of his when he got trapped in his attic. And I'll always remember the newspaper report of the man who had a heart attack and was incapacitated enough that he couldn't walk. But he yelled for help to his dog, who promptly brought the cell phone to him and saved his life.

Having mine within arm's reach has pulled me out of a scrape on several occasions after a car breakdown. The second time it happened was on a dark late night, far enough away from civilization that I just as well had been on the planet Pluto. It was on one of those boulevards with open fields on both sides of me. I was a mile or so from an industrial section and had it been necessary I could have hiked back to one of the businesses there, but that wouldn't have done any good because they were all closed. It was awfully reassuring to be holding that handful of plastic in my fist. And punching numbered buttons never felt better.

What a godsend cell phones have proven to be, whether one simply wishes to be more reachable or are lost in the woods, stranded in the sticks, or right in the middle of a natural disaster, like the Ohio woman who was caught in a sudden blizzard and got through to help just before her cell phone's battery went dead (a big lesson for keeping it charged).

Yes, it's nice to have a cell phone along any time you need it. But one rule I have made and never ever broken. It's what I call "the first cell phone commandment." I won't even think of using it while I am driving. I had made up my mind to that long before I even heard about the young woman who dropped her cell phone in the midst of a conversation while she was driving down the highway, reached down for it, and wound up losing her life when she smashed into a tree.

If you happen to be one of those intimidated by a cell phone, don't be. Any of the younger generation can help you learn its operation. All those extra frills aren't necessary to know, just the basics. In fact, all I've ever been concerned with is how to place and receive calls, program important numbers into it, and how to keep it charged. At the top of the numbers list, of course, is 9-1-1.

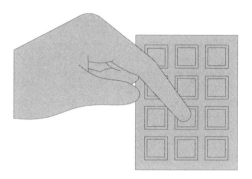

CHAPTER 13:

CONTINUING EDUCATION: MAKING A SMARTER YOU

You might consider investing some of your time pursuing a favorite subject or even exploring a new one.

After all, you're never to old to learn. Old dogs *can* learn new tricks. I proved that with Shadow when I taught him to roll over when he was well past puppy-hood. In fact, do we ever quit learning?

When you are young, there is nothing worse than school. A motivation close to zero encouraged me to look at my watch approximately every 5 minutes until the day's session was over, all the while trying to devise ways to get out of doing homework and invent excuses for not attending class. I lived for afternoons, weekends and holidays. That was reflected in my mediocre grades.

But what about now? Chances are your attitude is much different. I have certainly learned to value education.

I took a course many years ago in creative writing, when I felt I needed to sharpen my penmanship. Then much later on, just for fun I went back to school to gain more exposure to physical science. We learned about the solar system, molecules, energy, chemical reactions, electricity, magnetism, atomic structure, and the like. There were lots of interesting facts I should have learned as a child, or that I had since forgotten.

I'll always remember how the instructor, a broad-shouldered German, once during the term unmanufactured ice from a beaker of water by compressing the air in it. Also, we got to look into a microscope and study single cell life, things like paramecium, hydras and amoebas. I had the privilege of feeding one of the paramecium.

The composition of atoms fascinated me. It was particularly interesting to note that the flow of electrons of those atoms from one atom to the next was the function that made electricity possible. Also interesting was the motion of the trade winds and ocean currents, and the fantastic differences in the distances of stars and the wide variance in their colors.

Did you know that the sun's rays heat the equatorial seas, which expand and flow toward the poles, while the polar waters sink and flow toward the equator on the ocean floor? Did you know that even at the speed of light, it would require 4 and 1/2 years to reach the nearest star, Alpha Centauri?

Although I never planned to become a scientist, it was a course well worth taking. I was glad I invested the time. If nothing more, I figured I could use some of what I learned to impress my friends.

A college or university is also an excellent place to meet new people and perhaps gain a few friends. I met one dark-haired, heavy-set fellow while I was taking my science course who was fascinating. He was extremely analytical and related many details of which never had occurred to me on a variety of subjects. I pulled off a "B" in the course, but I would lay odds he earned an "A" with flying colors to boot. Maybe he should have been teaching the class.

At the suggestion of Phyllis, who thought I needed a change in my life (Was I getting crotchety?), I once enrolled in an art class, which largely covered how to make knickknacks and ornaments using colored glass. What convinced me to go through with it, however, had nothing to do with her, but it was an attraction to one of the colors—green. I figured I could make money by selling what I produced in art shows. I put together little sailboats, men fishermen with a catch on their line, and similar items.

The way it worked, I'd cut the shapes I needed from large sheets of the various colors of glass. I'd use a blue piece to represent water, a brown strip for the boat, and white pieces for sails. Then I would cover the edges with foil and solder the pieces into place. I had a thing about the men fishermen. I would also shape a human figure in a "straw" hat holding a fishing pole and attach a small fish-shaped piece for the catch, at the end of a strip of wire that represented the line. I did make a few bucks, but I was never very good at it. I hadn't inherited the art skills of my mother.

I remember two of the students quite well. One was a dark-haired, oval-faced young lady and the other a trim, sandy-haired young gentleman. They caught each others eyes from the beginning. On the last day of class, the instructor and his wife invited all us students to celebrate our "graduation" by going out for drinks. By then, the pair were inseparable. Just between you, me, the gate post—and maybe one other person, I suspect they tied the knot shortly thereafter. I'll always wonder. I wonder too how many married couples met under similar circumstances.

I recall hearing about one woman who took a computer science course. She learned a lot about word processing and spread sheets, but the thing that impressed her the most was when the instructor slipped by her and unplugged the computer she was working on to simulate a power failure. That taught her very early on to regularly save all her work.

There is a subject to interest everyone: history, science, health, mathematics, English literature, music, art, electronics, computer science, law, bar tending, psychology, and foreign language. And most of these choices can be broken down into more specific categories. In the field of math alone, there exists such categories as algebra, geometry, trigonometry, calculus and accounting. The field of science fans out into astronomy, biology, geology, chemistry, physiology, physics and the like. And just think how many languages there are.

Check accredited schools (universities, colleges or trade schools). If you find it too difficult to attend class regularly, consider a correspondence course. The internet is probably the best place to start.

CHAPTER 14:

BEING A VOLUNTEER: A GOOD TURN FOR THE COMMUNITY

I never did get into volunteer work as such, but the topic demands to be addressed. You might consider devoting some of your time to it. There are lots of opportunities whereby you can prove useful to your community, if not the world. In fact, this might just be the time to contribute something that you were too busy to in your younger days, when you were working hard to make a living, to raise a family.

According to the *Volunteering in America 2010 Issue Brief*, released by the Corporation for National and Community Service, 63.4 million Americans across the nation volunteered to help their communities in 2009, an increase of 1.6 million compared to the prior year. There are a number of nonprofit organizations that always need volunteers.

Foster Grandparents Plan is one such example.

Another is the Retired and Senior Volunteer Programs (RSVP), which includes the Foster Grandparents Plan, and also includes the Senior Companions Program that offers assistance and friendship to adults who are experiencing difficulties in daily living tasks, such as shopping and dressing themselves. RSVP also provides opportunity to tutor disturbed or disabled youths, organize neighborhood watch programs, assist in renovating homes, teach immigrants the English language, offer service in Homeland Security efforts, and assist victims of natural disasters. The website is www.seniorcorps.org.

SCORE is another possibility. It has supplied small business mentoring and training since 1964. It's a nonprofit organization with over 12,000 volunteers each year assisting in initiating almost 20,000 new businesses. Check www.score.org.

The Peace Corps is excellent if you are interested in public service abroad and your situation allows you the opportunity to relocate. Their website is www.peacecorps.gov.

Recording for the blind and dyslexic is another opportunity. If you like reading books, this might just be for you. Many over 65 are doing it. To find a studio in your area where you can record what you read, go to www.rfbd.org. They are especially interested in subjects such as accounting, chemistry, economics and medicine.

You can also find information on volunteering and community service at www.aarp.org.

Volunteering can be done independently as well. Check with your church or synagogue, or with local schools. You may be needed, for instance, to serve refreshments at social functions or help during times of renovation.

If would be good to volunteer, even if on appropriate occasions you just offer your services to someone you know. I helped a neighbor once build a room onto his house, and I was able to bang my thumb with the hammer twice. (Fortunately, I easily survived it.) My thumb might not have felt the best ever, but *I* did, knowing he really needed the help to finish before winter set in.

I also helped distribute flyers at the request of my sister who had a friend who was starting an irrigation business. The business had a successful launch and is still thriving today. In addition, I once passed out pamphlets for a local church. No pay on any of it, of course, but plenty of exercise and warm feelings.

If volunteering in any of these ways scares you, don't think you have to abandon the idea. Time is not the only thing that counts. You can also volunteer money or material goods, be it in the form of tithing, pledges or donations.

I came forward on this score in 2005 when the levee gave way in New Orleans after hurricane Katrina. I've also donated food and bottled water on several others occasions. Such deeds have never failed to make me feel good. I know I have done my part to help rescue others the way my friends have rescued me.

CHAPTER 15:

SECOND CAREERS

If volunteering fails to catch your fancy, perhaps your should consider the prospect of a second career—the kind of useful work with a pay check attached! Lots of older individuals have found lucrative and satisfying work long after their original careers ended.

Being what I deemed as active enough in retirement, I never went back to work at a regular job. (Although I'll admit my slight propensity for laziness might have influenced my judgment in this matter.) However, I made myself available on a temporary basis whenever my help was needed.

I pulled my sister's friend out of a jam when he started his irrigation business and helped him install a number of residential sprinkler systems until he got on his feet. Most of the time, things went well, but—as it always is with weather-dependent jobs—we did get caught in the rain several times, once in a downpour, which flooded the ditches that had been dug to lay the system of PVC pipes. We had to wait until the water had drained from the ditches and then were forced to work in the mud. It took us a week to complete a job that would have probably been finished by late the next day. Several other times, we were delayed when one of the workers accidentally cut a gas line while digging, those small orange plastic kind that connected to outdoor grills.

It was impossible to avoid getting glue all over your hands when gluing the pipe, but I caught on before very long and invested in a package of rubber gloves, those kind surgeons use. Needless to say, the job required a lot of squatting and stooping. It was hard work, but the pay was better than that for a professional couch potato and it helped soothe my aching muscles.

A few times when he had to leave town, a neighbor called me to be a fill-in manager for a Laundromat he owned. That wasn't nearly as hard, but on one occasion I had slipped away for a trip to the parts house to purchase a new starter switch for one of the dryers that had quit. While I was out, some wise guy came in and cut the hoses to nearly all the washing machines. You can imagine what fun I had replacing them all. But fortunately, things went along smoothly most of the time.

I also delivered newspapers a number of times for friends or their kids. Only once did I have any trouble and that was when it began to sleet unexpectedly. It wouldn't have been so bad if that particular route hadn't been loaded with hilly streets. But I survived and seldom got any complaints for a missed delivery.

The only other job I got involved with since retirement was that of cutting lawns. Occasionally, some of my neighbor's help failed to show and I found myself pushing a mower. A couple of times, we even threw in a little landscaping work as well. Of course, we got caught in a couple of good-sized rain showers during those times too. But it beefed up my pocketbook a little more while performing a good deed and, as in most of the other jobs, I got my quota of fresh air.

Some are quite the workhorse. There was a man who once retired from the towel supply company where I was seeking employment, enabling me to get his position, and was still there when I left the company 12 years later! That's right. He came out of retirement—not once, but twice during that interval and was still with the company for 6 months after I had left.

What was your line—health care, law enforcement, art and design, a managerial position, radio/TV, accounting/finance, marketing/communications? Most likely, you will have an interest in returning to it, since you already possess skills in that direction. But if you've had enough of your old job, you might consider an unrelated occupation—something that your other skills or interests will lead you toward.

There are many possibilities that could hold an interest for you that you may be able to qualify for, if necessary. Here are some examples:

Sales clerk (electronics outlets, department stores, etc.)

Delivery man (pies, milk, or whatever)

Ticket taker (theaters, sporting events)

Waiter at a restaurant

Vender (such as ice cream, or hot dogs and drinks, especially at sporting events where you can get a few peeks at the game for free)

Tailor

Lawyer

Cab driver

Truck driver

Announcer

Painter (not only house painting jobs, but ones that involve a canvas)

Cartoonist

Cook (furnishing you an excuse to indulge in a few extra nibbles)

Security guard

School crossing guard

Filling out income tax forms (a good work at your home job).

Design book covers or webpages (another good work at your home job).

Lay out advertisements (potentially another good work at your home job).

Teaching (Take advantage of your years of experience in your field and let your expertise help younger ones get the training they need.)

I knew a retired newspaperman who did quite well with vending machines. I can't say he made a killing, but he *did* put some extra money in his pocket. He managed a line of food and beverage machines for a number of years, and built up a route full of small businesses, eventually selling it for a profit.

Sometimes you can even make more money on a job than you did the first time around. I know of one jewelry salesman who did just that when he ventured out on his own after retiring and applied his know-how toward selling dental equipment. (Some guys have all the luck!)

If you are interested in going back to work, first determine what you have to offer. Then visit on-line educational sites to obtain information about any additional educational credentials you might require. Ask family and/or friends to put you in contact with people they know in the field you are seeking. You may want to visit www.second-careers.com.

CHAPTER 16:

MARRIAGE—AND RE-MARRIAGE

The one who said, "A woman's work is never done," knew what they were talking about. I bached it long enough to realize this and I think it helped me appreciate my wife a little more. In fact, I think that's the number one rule to remember to keep a marriage happy and in tack. And a happier marriage leads to a less grumpy person.

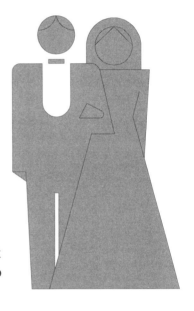

Too many men of our era are of the opinion, "Dear, all you have to do is wash a few dishes and clothes and put together a few meals and I have to *work* all day long." I once pictured it that way, but I changed my tune when I first had to fend for myself. I had to go to the store, cook (oh, how I hate that), do the banking, clean up after myself (I'm a messy person, despite my every effort to be otherwise), wash the clothes and vacuum the house, not to mention hold down a full-time job. (And I let the vacuuming job slide most of the time as it was.) Just doing the grocery shopping alone can take up a good hour, not counting the time it requires to put the food away. And I hate to even talk about the time and care it requires to prepare a decent meal. That, in fact, is the reason I ate out a good deal of the time while I was single. The point: What an insult it would be to you if after having labored faithfully all day long, your boss regarded your work as nothing at all.

So my rule numero uno for maintaining a happy marriage is "Never assume your wife is a slacker in regard to work." I've seen very few lazy women. They can't afford to be. If they jump off the work wagon for very long, they'll get so far behind they will never catch up. In fact, chances are that little woman has outworked you all her married life. What's more, men eventually retire, but not a woman. She can't afford to do *that* either. Learn to appreciate her for this, and by all means *tell* her you *do* appreciate her.

I also feel obligated to remind you that women are not objects of convenience. (Take it easy. I know you do know it; I'm just reminding you.) They're not just there to satisfy your stomach, wash the clothes, clean the house, and sew the button back on your favorite shirt. Nor are they designed to be a bed partner just when *you* have the urge. They have feelings just like you: desires, fears, favorite activities, concerns, pleasant memories, pet peeves and the like. They are human beings, friends for life, someone in whom you can confide as well as reassure, someone to cherish as well as someone to cherish you.

Before I list the rest of my rules for a happy marriage, here are a few facts that I have learned over the years about women that might be of help to you toward better appreciation of those rules. At least some of them you've probably already learned yourself, but here they are:

Women need to feel loved, needed and appreciated.

Women operate under the principle of feelings, not facts. They are more responsive to the question, "How do you feel about ------?" rather than "What do you think about ------?"

Women enjoy beautiful colors, and sweet fragrances—and they are fond of flowers, perfume, jewelry and delicate little knickknacks. (A good idea for gifts, wouldn't you say?)

Women are more fond of the romantic gifts such as flowers, candy, a music box or even a nightgown than they are a tool, a kitchen apparatus, or the like.

Women tend to be intuitive, which holds as much value, if not more so, as the "gut feelings" that a man occasionally experiences.

Wives are not the only ones who are imperfect. It may bruise the ego somewhat, but you fit into that same category. (*Don't* you?)

A woman has a fear of being less attractive to you after she has grown older and loves to be reassured that she is still beautiful in your eyes. (Well-placed compliments might prevent the birth of a grumpy old woman. But, then, this book is about grumpy old men, isn't it?—although a grumpy old woman might easily become the cause of a grumpy old man.)

Little gifts are perfectly adequate. They express love just as much as the big ones. Besides, it's not the gift but what's behind it that counts. (Just between you and me, it makes your pocketbook feel a little better, doesn't it?)

Now here are the rest of my rules for maintaining a happy marriage:

Become an expert at the art of apology. There's no reason why you shouldn't have already. You've had plenty of opportunity for practice, haven't you?

There's nothing that beats a hug and a kiss to heal a marital wound. The cost to you—nothing!

If you think she argues too much, be positive and consider it strong conviction. Save your vocal chords for more constructive matters—like yelling at the referees during an important ball game.

If you think she is spending too much money, regard it as an attempt to improve both of your life-styles. You might also privately pray that your bank balance stays in the black.

If she is expressing stubbornness, think of it as determination, resolve. After all, you've never been anything other than determined yourself— never stubborn.

Never compare your wife to another woman. They don't ever like it. They long for you to think that there is no other woman that comes close to being as wonderful for you as her—mothers included.

As stated above, reassure your wife that she still possesses beauty. If she shows you a new wrinkle or an age spot or mentions her expanding waistline, tell her something like, "You look more beautiful with each passing year." Or, "Your inner beauty gives you a radiance that catches my eye everyday."

Tell her you love her—regularly. Everyday wouldn't hurt.

Brag about her to your friends and family—in front of *her*, of course—or you will find yourself with only a hope that it gets back to her.

Be a good listener. Don't have your nose buried in the newspaper or eyes glued to the TV when she has something to say. Or don't try to get tricky and put up a good pretense by turning her way while daydreaming about your hobby or thinking about that ball game you saw last night.

Keep the lines of communication open. Did you ever try to talk into a disconnected phone (doing it when you were a kid doesn't count) or listen to a telephone conversation with the receiver on the hook?

There are times for togetherness and times to do your own thing. She requires time to herself just like you do. So it's O. K. to watch a football game by yourself—just don't forget that dinner date you made with her.

If you become angry, take some time to chill out. Retreat to your private corner—that special place that you consider more yours than hers—the basement workshop, the garage (not permitted during 20 degree weather), that wicker chair in the library, or the sofa in the living room.

Don't be a slob and make it any harder than necessary for her to clean up. Wipe up loose crumbs from the breakfast table, hang up clothes, and don't forget when you've just been outside and track mud onto the floors. (It's a surety that if you perform this last misdeed that carpet will have been freshly vacuumed.)

Never forget your wedding anniversary—even if you are sometimes tempted to do so because at the moment it feels as if you've been married forever.

Don't try to change her. Would you want her trying to change you? (Not that you need changing.)

Strive for compromise. Many disagreements have been solved by meeting each other halfway.

When you are happy, share the reason why with her. Who was it who said, "A joy shared is twice a joy"?

When she is angry, sympathize. Remember, "a grief shared is half a grief."

Steer away from pointing out her faults. (Thank goodness you don't have any faults that she could point out to *you*. Or *do* you?)

Accentuate her good points. (You might discover she has almost as many as you.)

Inject humor into your marriage. Find ways to generate a smile in her, if not a healthy laugh.

If she nags—there's only one thing you can do: Straighten up and fly right!

I could go on and on about my experiences with marriage. There were times I made mistakes and times I was glad I didn't. I once made a comment about why we had to have chicken two days in a row. Phyllis was under pressure at the time because of a sick mother, yet I still expected the best from her. I wondered why she got so miffed about such a "little thing" until I came to my senses later. You can bet I made one big apology. It wasn't a new-purple-outfit kind of apology, but was extensive enough to make room for a hug and a few kisses.

Sometimes it requires a shade of prompting to respect your wife's feelings. There was the time a lady told me that her husband wanted to go on a trip but she didn't much want to. She finally relented and said she was glad later, because her husband had since passed away. It was easy for me to reverse the roles in my mind. Shortly thereafter my wife wanted one of her quiet evenings a home with just the two of us, while I wanted to go out to a movie. We stayed home and although I was somewhat disappointed at the moment, I felt good about it later, assured that I had pleased her. I'll admit, I've slipped in the regard of respect all too often since then, but I think that brief conversation helped me to improve my track record.

Marriage can sometimes be a roller coaster. There are days you could run away with a perfect three-legged race and moments that one wrong word would bring tears. I remember this best being expressed by a joke I heard that went this way: "Some days I love my wife so much I could eat her up and the next day I wished I had."

But there's a lot to be said for marriage. Whether you fall ill with kidney stones, or fall *down* and break an ankle, someone is around, just as you are around for them. It's nice to have that partner in your life, too, during those challenging times, say, to reassure each other when the finances take a tumble or to support each other in the midst of the empty nest syndrome. And it's certainly good to have that companionship after a death in the family, especially if it happens to involve one of your offspring.

There will be arguments, sure, whether financial or political, or whether it concerns children, grandchildren or great grandchildren, the car or the house, or one of any number of decisions. But if both of you agreed about everything, one of you wouldn't be necessary in the relationship. You're not carbon copies. Perhaps this can best be summed up by Ellen Kreidman who states in her book *Light Her Fire,* "A fulfilling partnership with a woman is only possible when both of you realize that the other person may think and do things differently, but that each of you has equal value and that each of you must respect the other person's uniqueness."

And here's one additional thought. If you're fortunate enough to still have your woman, fine and good. But if you are once again single, you may be considering re-marriage. If so, do not be abashed at the prospect of re-marriage at any age. I had a 90-plus-year-old neighbor across the street who came within a whisker of doing just that.

That reminds me of a touching story about an 80-plus-year-old man residing in a senior care center who had never married because in his younger days he had lost who he considered to be his one and only. As it turned out, it was discovered that his very object of affection, who had also never entered the bonds of holy matrimony, was also residing in that same building on another floor. They were reunited and ultimately saw fit to tie the knot!

CHAPTER 17:

UNDERSCORING THE POSITIVES

True, the advancement in years brings about far too many negatives, but why not concentrate on the positives? Of all the things I've learned throughout my years, the one thing I think is the most important concerning attitude is to find two positive things for every negative one. Take a simple matter for instance. If the supermarket is out of your favorite flavor of ice cream and you walk away empty handed, at least you save a few bucks and probably avoid acquiring an extra pound as well. If searching for two positives is too much of a strain, try for one. There's always a silver lining somewhere.

Here are some of my one- and two-liners to get you in the positive mode:

There's no sin involved in spilling, only a mess.

You're never too old (oops, elderly) to learn.

You're not elderly, much less old; You're simply a senior citizen.

You won't get arrested by picturing yourself as a younger person, say, 50 . . . well, maybe 60.

As long as you can think of 95 as old, you're not so bad off.

Senior years bring greater experience. The older, the more experience.

There's no harm in thinking of birthdays as an excuse to eat ice cream and cake, rather than looking upon them as a reminder that you are one year older.

If you can still walk, be thankful you are mobile. If not, take note that a wheelchair prevents tired feet, besides getting you out of a lot of chores you don't care to be in on.

Here are some other things I have learned.

If I miss the first time and grope at the next three passes, I unabashedly try again. Eventually I know I'm going to get what I go after.

I try to laugh at my own mistakes and shortcomings—even if I accidentally drill a hole into my brand new table, which I once did. (I'll have to admit I wasn't laughing at the time, but that was a particularly hard one.) Later, however, I reminded myself to be grateful for the fact that at least I didn't drill the hole in my head.

I accept what I have to. If I can't open cellophane packaging bare-handed, I try the scissors. I know I don't have to be ashamed of it, but neither do I have to post the fact on the internet.

I've also discovered that it is helpful to lighten up. I remember reading somewhere about an older man who gave a list of things he would do if he could start his life over. One of the items on that list stood out to me. He said, "I would be sillier."

I also suggest you engage yourself in activities that help you try to recapture your childhood. It makes you feel younger. I went to the library one time and checked out "Treasure Island" and reread it. Many times I've pulled out one of my old video tapes and played an episode of a very old TV series or a ventage World War II movie. You could also watch cartoons, but don't let anyone see you doing it. (That would risk establishing a second childhood reputation.)

You certainly appreciate your situation when you hear about the tragedy in others lives. It's a relief to know that you weren't in the water in San Francisco when that shark attacked, that you weren't in Mexico City when that earthquake struck, or that you weren't aboard flight ----- which crashed in the Ozarks.

But misfortune carries more impact when it comes closer to home. I remember hearing of a man (an acquaintance of my parents, and someone who I had met) who headed off on a fishing trip with friends and while en route was injured in a serious automobile accident. I don't remember how badly the others were affected, but he had to have a pin inserted in his hip and it took him some time to recover as well as could be expected. Eventually, he and his buddies were up to taking off again to get that fishing excursion in, whereby they were involved in another serious accident. This time they walked away, and the man decided, "The Good Lord just didn't intend for me to go fishing." I'm certain his companions concurred.

I remember other friends of my parent's, who had been transferred way down to Corpus Christi, Texas. My mother found out later that they too had been involved in a automobile accident and their 5 year old daughter was seriously injured. The couple held onto hope for all of one hour, but it was no use. The little girl didn't survive. My heart really went out to them. Losing a child is bad enough as is sudden death, and the two combined don't make a good combination by any stretch.

An acquaintance of mine had a sobering experience once when he thought about an old friend he hadn't seen in several years and decided to phone him. The man's wife answered, sadly informing him that he had fallen victim to a heart attack a few days earlier and never recovered.

Finding the positive can certainly help you cope with misfortune of your own. In fact, when tragedy touches, it's difficult but essential that you find those positives. I was shocked when my dad, who always seemed to be in the best of health, had a heart attack. But I had to remind myself that it hadn't turned out to be fatal, and that the blockage in his arteries could be corrected with a bypass.

When my mother was laying in a hospital bed bad of cancer, I prayed ardently for her recovery. She had been an active person, writing song, painting pictures, zealous in the church, and enthusiastic about her friends. She tried harder than anyone I ever knew to hold onto life. I pondered over why some commit suicide while others struggle to stay alive. I wanted her to get well more than anything else. But when I realized it wasn't in the divine plan, I prayed that she be released from her suffering and God swiftly answered that prayer. As much as it hurt to lose her, I was grateful that her misery had been put behind her for good.

I was forced to deliver the message of her death to my father and sister. That wasn't pleasant either, but I had to remind myself that the rest of the family was alive and healthy, that we would all survive it as everyone else nearly also manages to do, and that I would one day see my mother again in a resurrection.

I was also grateful for the things she left behind for us: her book of poetry, tapes of music she had played, the hymns she had written, oil paintings, and all the little wooden knickknacks she had made for the many art shows she had signed up for. One of her paintings of Grand Teton still hangs on the living room wall, as well as a flowered design painted on a small fancily shaped plaque.

I experienced a similar situation to that of my mother's when late one night I began to think about my uncle who lived down Louisiana way. He had been coming to mind more often of late, but that night he was especially prevalent in my mind. The next morning my cousin called to tell me we had lost him. He had died in a senior care center while sitting in his chair. We counted our blessings that all the rest of the family members were well.

Near tragedy can work for the same purpose. I was once driving a pie delivery truck in a heavy rain along a divided, double-lane thoroughfare. To my right were office building and to the left was an employee parking lot. A young woman, already drenched, started running across the street to get to her office. There was another vehicle ahead of me in the other lane moving more slowly and she decided she had plenty of time to cross in front of it. But it blocked her view of me, and visibility was limited as it was. She ran right out into my path and I did the only thing I could do—make my best attempt to stop. Somehow I rolled to a halt mere inches from her body, as she screamed in horror. When I related the story to my employer, I could only conclude with: "I applied the brake and God stopped the truck."

I was glad that I had been able to avoid an accident that could have crippled or killed her. And I was equally thankful that I hadn't become a victim like she almost did. I imagine she had a lot to tell her co-workers that day.

Another time, the house got struck by lightning. It had been a cloudy day, but not a threatening one. It never even rained. We were just standing, innocently, unsuspecting, in the kitchen when the house was jarred by just about the loudest bang I ever remember. It curled the roof shingles, and burned out the garage door opener, the dish LNB and two of our telephones. Our insurance didn't cover all the damage, but we were grateful that we hadn't been outside at the time. Only our pocketbook was hit, not us.

One more thing I will add to help you accentuate the positive. Don't look toward the future with an attitude of worry. When has any man ever added one cubit to his stature by doing so? I've been guilty far too often in the past of fretting over a matter that never even came to be, or over a situation that turned out not to be nearly as serious as I had anticipated. Whether it involves a medical procedure you are to soon undergo, or the fact that your son's marriage may terminate, at least wait until the concern comes and deal with it then. And I doubt that there is any reason to agonize over the possibility of running out of money to live on. I don't know anyone personally who ever has. Instead, keep in mind the things you look forward to, such as an upcoming visit by the grandchildren, your next round of golf, the next ball game on TV, or for that matter the dinner your wife is cooking.

Likewise, forget the regrets from the past. Why expend any grief over the fact that you overreacted to your wife's minor fender-bender the week before, or that you didn't get what you expected out of your insurance company when the house sustained damage from a storm a month earlier, or that you didn't get that raise on your last social security check? Why keep concerning yourself over the quarrel you had with that friend 3 years ago? What's the use in doting over the mistakes you might have made with your children, or allowing yourself to feel blue for the times your kids disappointed you? Instead, when thinking back (whether the focus is 2 days ago or 50 years), hold onto fond memories: the good times you've had with the grandchildren, the joy you experienced when your local team won the championship last season, the satisfaction you received from achievements, or the fun you had on trips.

There is only one other possibility to consider—the present. Apply most of your concentration there, since that's where you are anyway. Make the very most of it and be grateful you are still here to enjoy it.

This should encourage you to underscore the positives in your life. In fact, why not go all out and print them in your mind in big red letters? That's what baseball great Lou Gehrig must have done when, despite his serious affliction, he said, "...I consider myself the luckiest man on the face of the earth."

CHAPTER 18:

THINGS I WANT TO DO WHILE I'M STILL TICKING AND KICKING

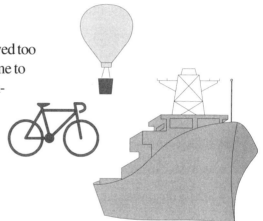

Now that life's gas gauge has moved too far to the left to suit me, I figure it's time to consider things I have always had a hankering to do all my life—things I've never done before—including the extraordinary, even the downright unreasonable. (Hey, if you are going to wish, why set boundaries?) Here's my list:

- Run the country for 1 year. Well, 1 month, anyway. O. K., then, at least 1 week.

- Take a swim in the Dead Sea. (I want to make sure it's salty enough to keep me from sinking.)

- Ice skate without falling.

- Live in a mansion for one whole month—better still, *own* the mansion.

- Live in a house with a mountain view.

- Build a house from scratch—just the way my wife and I want it.

- Take a tour of a castle.

- Search for treasure and actually find it.

- Read *War and Peace*.

- Hang a cabinet without it turning out to look crooked.

- Tear a telephone book in half—bare-handed, of course.
- Lift 300 pounds.
- Teach a dog to talk.
- Cash in on a skyrocketing stock.
- Win the lottery.
- Kayak somewhere along the Mississippi River.
- Take a hike in the Grand Canyon.
- Take a trip to Hawaii.
- Take a trip to Alaska.
- Visit Venice, Italy.
- Go fishing in the Indian Ocean.
- Bring back a souvenir from the Orient.
- Take a cruise in the Caribbean.
- Make a trip around the world (in less than 80 days).
- Spend an entire winter in Equador.
- Grow a green thumb.
- Repair a TV set.
- Tame a wild horse.
- Build a ship in a bottle (or, what the heck, why not be imaginative and build a space shuttle in the bottle).
- Become a star quarterback for the Oakland Raiders.
- Pitch in a World Series.
- Make sense of the income tax form.
- Convince at least one person to stop smoking.
- Buy a wide-screen TV.
- Play the lead role in a movie. (Actually, I'll settle for a bit part, just as long as I can say I appeared in the movie.)

- Be the star of my own prime time sitcom (or at least one of the regular cast members).

- Be the lead character in a play. (or at least play the second role)

- Bowl a 300 game.

- Catch a record catfish.

- Get a hole in one on the toughest course there is (miniature golf not included).

- Learn Spanish.

- Learn French.

- Learn to play the piano.

- Learn to play the guitar.

- Learn how to create a decent webpage.

- Take a bike tour.

- Ride on a wagon train.

- Be a successful stand-up comedian.

- Help some aspiring person to become a successful writer.

- Launch what would become a successful business.

- Walk as far as I want without getting tired.

- Sky dive—on a clear day, of course.

- Skin dive in the Mediterranean.

- Win the Pulitzer Prize.

- Win the Nobel Prize.

- Spit from the top of the Eiffel Tower.

- Drop a ball off the Leaning Tower of Pisa.

- Travel on a river boat (you know, those old-timers with a paddle wheel).

- Ride a camel (even if it's only in my backyard).

- Be a passenger aboard a submarine.

- Start a fire by rubbing two sticks together.

- Invent something—especially if it revolutionizes the world, like, say, a drug to cure cancer.

- Discover something of monumental importance.
- Win the world over to Christianity.
- Live long enough to become a great grandfather.
- Sip sherry in Acapulco.
- Climb a mountain (a real mountain, not a mole hill).
- Be the one to produce another Star Trek series.
- Watch every single episode of *Gunsmoke*.
- Convince a child to love school.
- Win a contest.
- Ride a motorcycle around the block.
- Teach an elephant a trick.
- Own a cabin in the woods.
- Own a Rolls-Royce.
- Become an expert cook.
- Break open a coconut without making a mess.
- Eat dinner 3 days in a row without a salesman calling. (Actually I think I've managed that a few times, so this one may not count.)
- Draw a royal flush is a poker game—especially one with high stakes.
- Eat all I want of all the foods I am allergic to—without ill effects.
- Become a crackerjack orator
- Appear on talk shows and become famous.
- Figure out a complex mathematical formula without the use of a calculator.
- Find a three-legged buffalo nickel.
- Find a three-leaf glover.
- Find a two-headed lizard.
- Go skiing in the Alps.
- Own a persimmon tree.
- Grow more hair.

- Drive a limousine.
- Write my very own computer program.
- Write a song—especially one that turns out to be a hit.
- Grant one wish to every member of the family.
- Set sail in my very own schooner.
- Ride in a helicopter.
- Ride a hot-air balloon above Big Sur
- Ride in a dirigible somewhere along the west coast.
- Go surfing in the Pacific.
- Witness a baseball triple play.
- Have the key to a city for 1 day.
- Visit at least one African nation.
- Drive a fire truck—not to a fire, just around the block a couple of times— with the siren blaring.
- Drive a police car—with siren at full blast so I can run as many red lights as I want.
- Ride on a double-decker bus.
- Drive a stagecoach.
- Brand a steer.
- Take a peek at the Andromeda Galaxy through the telescope at Mount Wilson Observatory.
- See the planet Pluto through a telescope—so I won't have to say it's the only planet I haven't seen.
- See the Northern Lights.
- Spend a few days on a deserted island while I read *Swiss Family Robinson*.
- Fly in a vintage aircraft.
- Own an oil well—one that produces, of course.
- Bend steal in my bare hands (even a thin, defective piece).

- Walk in space.
- Fly like Peter Pan.
- Meet an astronaut.
- Take a ride in a space shuttle (Better still, learn to pilot one).
- Set foot on the moon.
- Be the first man on Mars.
- Turn back the clock and start all over!

CHAPTER 19:

BOWING OUT: WHEN IT'S TIME TO SAY "DIE"

There is a certain sense of urgency as we get old enough. It's a time when we think about wills and falls on the concrete, not to mention heart attacks and strokes. It's an age when we ponder over regrets, and wish we could begin life anew. Yet we assume that we will awake into the next day, and it is our hope that we'll be around to experience at least one more football season, another birthday, and one more vacation.

Death is a subject that at this stage of life is more often than not avoided. I certainly don't want to bow out just yet, and I can't help hoping that medical science will figure a way to extend life more. Even an extra 10 years are so wouldn't be bad.

But there comes a time everyone must take a bow and exit. It makes little difference whether it happens as it did with Bing Crosby, who dropped dead at the golf course in the middle of a game, or as with the man I remember hearing about many years ago who died while sitting in church. Nor does it matter whether your life ends in an automobile crash or you take your last breath in bed. Death is death.

There's one good thing about death. You don't know that date and time. If you knew you were to depart life on the 28th of_____, you'd soon be squirming and you certainly wouldn't feel very cheerful on the 27th!

My philosophy is to play off of that positive with other positives. Rather than allowing the black veil of worry to smother me over this issue, I focus on those accomplishments I made in life: the family I've raised and the books I've written, for instance. And I also draw off of the many pleasant memories: the trips I've shared with the family, the love I've given and received, and the things I've done with friends. And I'm glad even more than ever for the favors I had the opportunity to do for others, not that it's been nearly enough.

I also must tell you how it has helped me by not neglecting the spiritual side of life. You don't have to set aside just one day a week to regard religious matters by assembling in a house of worship. I start each day out by reading the Bible. It's the first thing I do in the morning, before breakfast even. I read one chapter and it only requires a short time. I feel like I do a lot better during each day because it sets the tone. There's nothing like the way it informs and comforts.

I've not only found comfort from the Bible but from prayer as well. I know God is there for me as He is with all of us. He has answered many of my prayers in the positive, and on those times I didn't get what I asked for, I can look back and see how I eventually got something I wanted even more. Just thanking Him for a multitude of blessings have helped me refresh my memory about the positives in my life, which distracts me from the dread of death.

Don't let your ego tell you that religion is mostly for women and kids. To me, it's the most vital element for coping with death. When I get to pondering on the subject, I go back and read John 5:28 and Acts 24:15, and thank God for His promise of a resurrection. Then I tell myself, until death does take place, there is a life to be lived.

CHAPTER 20:

CONCLUSION FROM A GRUMPY OLD MAN WHO HAS LEARNED NOT TO BE SO GRUMPY

From all that I've brought forth in these pages, I hope you see how I have learned to accept old age with grace.

I've done what needs to be done to take care of myself and focused on the positives. (Agility has not abandoned me. My auditory senses are still acute. Pains are relatively few. And I don't have to wear false teeth.)

I also keep active with the things I enjoy (writing, collecting things, reading, taking trips), as well as jump whenever I'm called to do a favor for my family, a friend, a neighbor, or even a stranger, grateful that I am able to do so. And I have not shunned religious matters.

I really don't mind so much being this old. Now I hope you don't either.

To sum it all up, perhaps it's best to adopt the attitude of Mark Twain, who once said, "Age is an issue of mind over matter. If you don't mind, it doesn't matter."